1,000,000 Books

are available to read at

www.ForgottenBooks.com

Read online
Download PDF
Purchase in print

ISBN 978-1-332-11202-9
PIBN 10286190

This book is a reproduction of an important historical work. Forgotten Books uses state-of-the-art technology to digitally reconstruct the work, preserving the original format whilst repairing imperfections present in the aged copy. In rare cases, an imperfection in the original, such as a blemish or missing page, may be replicated in our edition. We do, however, repair the vast majority of imperfections successfully; any imperfections that remain are intentionally left to preserve the state of such historical works.

Forgotten Books is a registered trademark of FB &c Ltd.
Copyright © 2018 FB &c Ltd.
FB &c Ltd, Dalton House, 60 Windsor Avenue, London, SW19 2RR.
Company number 08720141. Registered in England and Wales.

For support please visit www.forgottenbooks.com

1 MONTH OF
FREE
READING

at

www.ForgottenBooks.com

By purchasing this book you are eligible for one month membership to ForgottenBooks.com, giving you unlimited access to our entire collection of over 1,000,000 titles via our web site and mobile apps.

To claim your free month visit:

www.forgottenbooks.com/free286190

* Offer is valid for 45 days from date of purchase. Terms and conditions apply.

English
Français
Deutsche
Italiano
Español
Português

www.forgottenbooks.com

Mythology Photography **Fiction**
Fishing Christianity **Art** Cooking
Essays Buddhism Freemasonry
Medicine **Biology** Music **Ancient
Egypt** Evolution Carpentry Physics
Dance Geology **Mathematics** Fitness
Shakespeare **Folklore** Yoga Marketing
Confidence Immortality Biographies
Poetry **Psychology** Witchcraft
Electronics Chemistry History **Law**
Accounting **Philosophy** Anthropology
Alchemy Drama Quantum Mechanics
Atheism Sexual Health **Ancient History**
Entrepreneurship Languages Sport
Paleontology Needlework Islam
Metaphysics Investment Archaeology
Parenting Statistics Criminology
Motivational

BOSCOBEL

OR THE HISTORY OF THE MOST MIRACULOUS PRESERVATION OF

KING CHARLES II.

AFTER THE BATTLE OF WORCESTER

SEPTEMBER THE THIRD

1651

BY THOMAS BLOUNT

To which is added the KING's own account of his adventures, dictated to Mr. SAMUEL PEPYS

EDITED WITH AN INTRODUCTION
AND BIBLIOGRAPHY BY
CHARLES G. THOMAS

WITH AN ARMORIAL FRONTISPIECE BY
C. W. SHERBORN

LONDON
TYLSTON AND EDWARDS
1894

BOSCOBEL

OR THE HISTORY OF THE MOST MIRACULOUS PRESERVATION OF

KING CHARLES II.

AFTER THE BATTLE OF WORCESTER SEPTEMBER THE THIRD 1651

BY THOMAS BLOUNT

To which is added the KING's own account of his adventures, dictated to Mr. SAMUEL PEPYS

EDITED WITH AN INTRODUCTION
AND BIBLIOGRAPHY BY
CHARLES G. THOMAS

WITH AN ARMORIAL FRONTISPIECE BY
C. W. SHERBORN

LONDON
TYLSTON AND EDWARDS
1894

Of this edition 500 copies have been printed

CONTENTS

INTRODUCTION

On September the 3rd, 1651, was fought at Worcester the last battle of the Civil War. A few weeks earlier Charles the Second had suddenly broken up his camp at Stirling and had crossed the Border at the head of 12,000 men, in the desperate hope of raising England against the Parliament. Meeting with little opposition on his march southward, but with no success in the enlistment of recruits, he occupied Worcester on August the 22nd, and on the following day was proclaimed king. On the 28th, Cromwell, who had followed rapidly from Scotland, appeared before Worcester with 30,000 men, and five days later, on the anniversary of Dunbar,—his lucky day—assaulted the city with overwhelming force. All day and far into the night the fight went on.

b

The overthrow of the Royalist army was complete: it is said that 3000 men were killed, and 5000 taken prisoners. Late in the evening, after a gallant but fruitless attempt to rally his broken forces, Charles rode off on the road to Kidderminster with sixty of his most trusty adherents.

The story of his subsequent adventures is, perhaps, the most romantic episode in the chequered history of the House of Stuart. No pains were spared by the Parliament to effect his capture. A reward of £1000 was offered for his apprehension; those who should harbour or assist him in any way were proclaimed guilty of high treason; magistrates were ordered to arrest all unknown persons found within their jurisdiction; and a strict watch was kept on the passages of rivers and at the sea-port towns. Nevertheless, Charles vanished so completely, that before the tidings came of his safe arrival in France, it was currently believed that after his flight from

Worcester he had been killed by peasants ignorant of his rank.

Something he owed to the route which chance led him to take. The common opinion was that he would endeavour to retreat to Scotland with the remnant of the army he had brought thence. Six days after the battle Colonel Birch wrote from Manchester to the Speaker of the House of Commons :

'I think the Scots' king came this way with 'Lieutenant-General Lesley and Lieutenant-'General Middleton, who were taken on Black-'stone Edge in the moors betwixt Karsdale and 'Halifax, and we believe that he escaped towards 'Yorkshire in some disguise. All search is 'made for him here that may be amongst the 'prisoners, but he cannot be heard of.'

Charles, however, had quickly decided that to retreat northward with a band of beaten and demoralised men was to court capture or destruction. His first plan was to push on with a few companions for London in the hope of arriving there before the news of his defeat. Finding this impossible, and being foiled in his subsequent design of reaching Wales by the difficulty of crossing the Severn, he journeyed in the disguise of a countryman southward into Somersetshire. On the failure of a well-planned attempt to embark at Charmouth, he determined to make for one of the south coast ports, and passing safely through Dorsetshire and Hampshire, finally set sail at Shoreham for the coast of Normandy, six weeks after the rout at Worcester.

But his deliverance was due mainly to that extraordinary personal devotion which the Stuarts inspired. The Prince Charles Edward was not more loyally served a century later by the clansmen of the Western Isles than was Charles the Second by the hinds and squires of Shropshire and Somerset. Forty or fifty persons were privy to his secret; but no individual was tempted by the greatness of the reward or the favour of a powerful Government to betray him. And in the personal courage he displayed, in his ready wit and good humour in suffering and danger, Charles bore himself not unworthy of the fidelity of his followers.

It is no wonder that so brave a tale of hair-breadth escapes and unswerving loyalties should have caught the popular fancy. In many a village there lingers to this day some tradition of the royal fugitive, and many a manor house is anxious to assert its claim to have sheltered him. The sign of 'The Royal Oak' still swings on numerous village inns, recalling that miserable day spent in the woods of Boscobel. To the fervid loyalists of the Restoration the story of the 'Royal Progress' was more strange and fascinating than a fairy tale. In the days of that great reaction, no flavour of servility was too strong; and of the accounts then published of the King's adventures some are written in a style which in our more sober century seems exaggerated and unmanly. Of these contemporary narratives the most satisfactory and complete is *Boscobel*, by Thomas Blount. It was popular at the time of its appearance, passed through many editions, and was translated into French and Portuguese. It is no doubt in the main an accurate account of what occurred; and it is in substantial agreement with the King's own story of his adventures, dictated by his majesty to Mr. Samuel Pepys at Newmarket in 1680.

Thomas Blount, born in 1618, was the son of Myles Blount of Orleton in Herefordshire, and came of a younger branch of the ancient family of his name. He was called to the Bar at the Inner Temple, and was the author of several works on legal subjects, the best known of which is *Fragmenta Antiquitatis: Ancient Tenures of Land and Jocular Customs of some Manors*, which appeared in 1679, and has been frequently republished. He died in 1679, aged sixty-one. In religion he was a Catholic.

The learned Dr. Nash, the historian of Worcestershire, denied that Blount was the author of *Boscobel*; but it has been commonly attributed to him, and the preface to the first edition of 1660 is signed Thomas Blount. He was undoubtedly familiar with the details of Charles's escape, and in his *Animadversions upon Sir Richard Baker's Chronicle and its Continuation*, published at Oxford in 1672, makes some parade of this knowledge. For example, the *Chronicle* says, 'His majesty by ladders ascended ' into the top of that most celebrated oake':—on which Blount remarks, 'There were no ladders ' in the case, for the King ascended the oake by ' the help of Colonel Carlos and two of the ' Pendrels and his own agility.'

The first part of *Boscobel*, printed for Henry Seile, London, 1660, contains an account of the King's adventures, up to the time of his leaving Boscobel. In 1681 a second part was published concluding the story. With the two parts was printed the *Claustrum Regale Reseratum*, by Mrs. Anne Wyndham, a narrative of the King's concealment at Trent in Somersetshire, which had previously appeared alone in 1667. A list of the various editions of these works is given below.

The King's own account, dictated to Mr. Samuel Pepys, and to be found among the Pepys MSS., is a singularly unaffected narrative and bears strong internal evidence of its genuineness. It is printed here in addition to *Boscobel*. From a comparison of the two the following diary of Charles's movements has been constructed.

Sept. 3rd. Battle of Worcester.

,, 4th. Charles reaches White Ladies in the early dawn; proceeds at night to Madeley and sleeps in a barn.

,, 5th. In the evening he returns to Boscobel,

,, 6th. and arrives there about 6 A.M. He conceals himself with Colonel Carlis in an oak during the day; in the evening sups at Boscobel House and sleeps there.

,, 7th. At nightfall he sets out for Moseley, accompanied by the Penderels and

Yates ; and is welcomed at Moseley by Mr. Whitgreave.

Sept. 8th. Boscobel is searched by Parliamentary troops. Charles remains at Moseley.

„ 9th. Moseley is visited by soldiers. Charles hides in a garret, and proceeds in the evening to Bentley Hall.

„ 10th. At dawn he leaves Bentley Hall, riding before Mrs. Jane Lane as a servant. At Wotton he rides through a troop of cavalry. The party sleeps at Mr. Tombs' at Long Marston ; and

„ 11th. proceeds to Cirencester.

„ 12th. Thence to Mr. Morton's house at Abbot's Leigh, near Bristol, where Charles remains till the 16th.

„ 16th. Finding no opportunity of embarking at Bristol, Charles sets out for Trent, in Somersetshire, the seat of Colonel Wyndham. He sleeps at Castle Cary.

„ 17th. He arrives at Trent, and remains there while Colonel Wyndham and Ellesdon endeavour to procure a vessel at Charmouth.

„ 22nd. The royal party proceeds thither. Failure of the attempt to take ship there.

Sept. 23rd. Charles having determined to return to Trent, sets forth for Bridport, and proceeds thence to Broadwindsor.

  ,,   24*th.* He reaches Trent in safety, and remains there till October 6th.

Oct.   6*th.* Charles leaves Trent in the morning, reaches Hele House, near Amesbury, the seat of Mr. Hyde, and remains there till the 13th.

  ,,   13*th.* He proceeds to Hambledon, in Hampshire, and sleeps at Mr. Symon's house.

  ,,   14*th.* He reaches Brighthelmstone;

  ,,   15*th.* Sets sail from Shoreham,

  ,,   16*th.* and arrives in safety at Fescamp, near Dieppe.

Around what may be termed the orthodox history, represented by Blount, the Pepys MS., and some of the minor narratives, there clusters a number of traditions and stories which must for the most part be pronounced apocryphal. Scott took Charles to Woodstock, Ainsworth to Ovingdean Grange;—for these flights of fancy there is of course no historical foundation. But as to the precise locality of various adventures

and incidents there is some diversity of opinion
in the more serious accounts, and still more in
popular tradition. This is not unnatural, as
until the Restoration, nine years later, it was
the interest of all concerned to keep secret the
part they had played. Some of the particulars
of the story seem to have leaked out, but it was
commonly thought that Charles had reached
London and embarked there. In the British
Museum is preserved a broadsheet entitled ' A
' mad Designe; or, a Description of the King of
' Scots marching in disguise after the rout at
' Worcester, with the particulars where he was,
' and what he and his company did every day and
' night after he fled from Worcester.' London,
printed by Robert Ibbitson, 1651; with
'November 6th' below in MS. In this Roundhead account it is related that Charles with the
Duke of Buckingham and Lord Wilmot came
into Cheshire and thence into the borders of
Lancashire, where they 'lay close in a hollow

'tree'; and that they obtained the assistance of a certain lady whose servants they pretended to be. 'On the ninth of September they took an 'intended voyage for Bristol, and the Scots' king 'rid before the lady on one horse, the Duke of 'Buckingham before her gentlewoman upon 'another horse, and the Lord Wilmot as her 'groom upon an horse by himselfe.

'About the middle of September they got to 'Bristol, but they heard in their inne so great 'a talk what search was made after them, that 'they presently took horse, not daring to stay 'there, and away they came for London.

'About the twentyeth of September they got 'to London, and went abroad, sometimes in the 'mornings and at evenings, but generally lay 'very close all day. . . .

'The Lord Wilmot procured a merchant to 'hire a ship of forty tuns to transport them, 'which cost them £120.

'About the middle of October, having taken

'leave of and thanked the lady with many
'salutations and promises, to Gravesend they
'went, and from thence on and a-shipboard
'. . . and so set saile for Havre de Grace,
'where they landed.'

There is also in the British Museum a ballad
of the same period entitled 'The last news from
'France; being a true relation of the escape of
'the King of Scots from Worcester to London,
'and from London to France, who was conveyed
'away by a young gentleman in woman's apparel;
'the King of Scots attending on this supposed
'gentlewoman in manner of a serving-man.'

A story is still current in Dorsetshire of
Charles having taken refuge in Coaxden Hall
between Chard and Axminster, and of his being
concealed there by Mrs. Cogan, the lady of the
house. It was first printed in Mr. Walter
Wilson's *Life and Times of Daniel Defoe*
(London, 1830), whose version is as follows:—
'Here they (the Cogans) were seated at the

' time of the battle of Worcester, when the
' Royalists being entirely defeated, Prince
' Charles, afterwards Charles II., escaped in
' disguise and for some weeks eluded his pursuers,
' until he found means to depart the country.
' Having gone to Lyme for that purpose, the
' people, who were most disaffected to him, soon
' got scent of it, which obliged him to make a
' hasty retreat. Closely pursued on all sides,
' he took refuge at Coaxden, and entering the
' parlour where Mrs. Cogan was sitting alone,
' threw himself upon her protection. It was
' then the fashion, as it was long afterwards,
' for ladies to wear large hoops; and as no time
' was to be lost, the soldiers being at his heels,
' she hastily concealed him under this portion
' of her dress. Mrs. Cogan was in her affections
' a loyalist, but her husband belonged to the
' opposite party, and was then out on his estate.
' . . . The lady provided for the security of
' the fugitive, until it was prudent for him to

' depart; and having furnished him with pro-
' visions and a change of apparel he proceeded
' on his journey to Trent.' .

It is added that Charles sent to Mrs. Cogan
from the Continent, as a reward for her loyalty,
a gold chain and locket engraved with his arms,
which remained in the family for over a hundred
years. It is strange that so striking a story,
if true, should not have found its way into any
of the contemporary accounts.[1] The conjecture
may be hazarded that Coaxden was one of the
numerous houses searched by Parliamentary
soldiers, and that Mrs. Cogan was wrongly
accused of concealing the fugitive in. the manner

[1] See 'King Charles the Second and the Cogans of Coaxden
Manor: A missing chapter in the *Boscobel Tracts*. Edited by a
Fellow of the Society of Antiquaries.' London: Elliot Stock,
1891. Also *Notes and Queries for Somerset and Dorset*, vol.
iii. part xxiv. Sherborne, December 1893.

A supposed visit of Charles to Pillesden House, Dorset, the
seat of Sir Hugh Wyndham, is dealt with in the *Proceedings
of the Dorset Natural History and Antiquarian Field Club*,
vol. vii. pp. 9-28.

described. It is quite possible that Charles sent her the chain as a recompense for indignities she may have undergone. At Pillesden House, in the neighbourhood, a young lady was cruelly treated under the belief that she was the king in disguise.

At his restoration, Charles lost no time in rewarding the chief actors in the drama of his escape. The Penderels—'five faithful brothers'—were summoned to Westminster, and received a suitable reward; and subsequently small pensions were settled on them and their heirs for ever. On Mrs. Jane Lane (afterwards Lady Fisher) a pension of £1000 a year for life was bestowed, and on her brother, Colonel Lane, one of £500. Smaller pensions were also granted to Dame Anne Wyndham, Mr. Whitgreave, Captain Tettersell, and others. To Colonel Carlis, Charles' companion in 'that most celebrated oake' at Boscobel, a grant of arms was made *in perpetuam rei memoriam.*

BIBLIOGRAPHY

THE following is a list of the contemporary narratives of Charles' escape. They may be divided into two classes : (1) those which give, or profess to give, a complete account of his proceedings; (2) subsidiary accounts of special periods or incidents, written by the chief actors themselves. In the former class the narratives of Charles himself, of Blount, and of Clarendon are the most important.

In the second class are comprised the Prisoner at Chester's letter, relating to the fight at Worcester; the narratives of Mr. Whitgrave and Father Huddleston; the 'Claustrum Regale Reseratum; or, the King's Concealment at Trent'; the accounts given by Mr. Ellison and Captain Alford of the attempted Embarkation at Charmouth; and Colonel Gounter's narrative of the last stage in the journey and the successful passage to Normandy. These minor histories are of great interest and importance, and a reprint of them would form a desirable supplement to the present volume.

In 1830 Mr. J. Hughes published a work entitled *The Boscobel Tracts*, in which were printed 'Boscobel,' the Pepys account, extracts from Clarendon, and some of the smaller narratives, with a valuable introduction. But Mr. Hughes does not seem to have been aware of the full extent of the literature of the subject. A second edition was published in 1857.

Among more recent publications may be mentioned *Captain Tettersell, and the Escape of Charles II.*, by F. E. Sawyer, Esq., Lewes, 1882—a pamphlet relating to the King's embarkation at Brighton, and the subsequent career of Captain Tettersell; and an interesting article entitled 'Boscobel and Whiteladies,' by Mr. J. Penderel-Brodhurst, a descendant of the Penderel family, which appeared in the *Art Journal* for 1889.

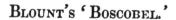
BLOUNT'S 'BOSCOBEL.'

—— Boscobel; or, the History of His Majestie's most miraculous Preservation after the Battle of Worcester, 3rd Sept. 1651. London. Printed for H. Seile, Stationer to the King's Most Excellent Majesty. 1660. 12mo, pp. 55.

—— Boscobel; or, the History of His Majestie's most miraculous Preservation after the Battle of Worcester, 3rd Sept. 1651, introduced by an exact relation of that battle, and illustrated with a map of the City. London. Printed for A. Seile, over against St. Dunstan's Church, in Fleet Street. 1662. 12mo, pp. 71.
   With this was published
—— Boscobel, etc. The Second Part. 12mo, pp. 38.

—— Boscobel, etc. The Third Edition, with addition of 'Claustrum Regale Reseratum; or, the King's Concealment at Trent.' Published by A. W. London. Printed by M. Clarke, and to be sold by H. Brome and C. Harper at their shops in St. Paul's Church Yard and Fleet Street. 1680. 12mo.

—— Boscobel, etc. The Fourth Edition. Edinburgh. Printed by James Watson, on the north side of the Cross, for Charles Jackson, merchant. 1709. 12mo, pp. vi. + 60. [Contains the two parts and the 'Claustrum.']

BLOUNT'S ' BOSCOBEL.'

—— Boscobel ; or, the Compleat History of the most miraculous Preservation of King Charles II. after the Battle of Worcester, September the 3rd, 1651, to which is added, 'Claustrum Regale Reseratum ; or, the King's Concealment at Trent.' Publish'd by Mrs. Anne Wyndham. The Fourth Edition, adorn'd with Cuts. With a Supplement to the whole. London. Printed for J. Wilford at the Three Golden Flower-de-Luces in Little Britain. MDCCXXV. 12mo, pp. 189.

—— Boscobel ; or, the Compleat History of the most miraculous Preservation of King Charles II. after the Battle of Worcester, April (*sic.*) the 3rd, 1651. To which is added, 'Claustrum Regale Reseratum ; or, the King's Concealment at Trent.' Publish'd by Mrs. Anne Wyndham. The Fifth Edition. With a Supplement to the whole. London. Printed for M. Cooper at the Globe, in Paternoster Row. MDCCXLIII. 12mo, pp. 192.

Another edition was published in 1769. In 1786 a reprint of the two parts of 'Boscobel' alone was published at Birmingham (printed for C. Earl. 8vo, pp. 132). A reprint of the First Edition of 1660 (the first part only) was published at Doncaster in 1809, and a similar reprint at Wellington, Salop, in 1822. Both parts of 'Boscobel' were printed by Mr. Hughes in the 'Boscobel Tracts,' 1830 and 1857.

THE KING'S ACCOUNT, DICTATED TO SAMUEL PEPYS.

An Account of the Preservation of King Charles II. after the Battle of Worcester, drawn up by himself. To which are added his letters to several persons. London, W. Sandby. 1766. 8vo, pp. viii. + 190.

To this narrative Mr. Pepys has subjoined his own remarks, and many corrections and illustrations procured from the King, from Father Hodlestone, and from Colonel Philips. They are inserted in the form of notes.

—— An Account, etc. Glasgow. Printed by Robert and Andrew Foulis, and sold by John Balfour, Bookseller in Edinburgh. MDCCLXVI. Small 8vo, pp. 190.

—— The same sheets with a new imprint. Edinburgh. Printed for Archibald Constable, by J. Moir, Royal Bank Close, 1801. Also in London, printed for S. Gosnell, 1803.

—— An Account of King Charles the Second's escape from Worcester, dictated by the King himself. From the Pepys MSS. In the *Bibliotheca Curiosa* of E. M. Goldsmid. 1883. 8vo, pp. 42.

This Account is printed in Hughes' 'Boscobel Tracts.'

CLARENDON (LORD). HISTORY OF THE REBELLION (13TH BOOK).

'Clarendon professed to have derived his information from Charles and the other actors in the transaction, and asserts that "it is exactly true;

that there is nothing in it the verity whereof can justly be suspected." Yet whoever will compare it with the other accounts will see that much of great interest has been omitted, and much so disfigured as to bear little resemblance to the truth. It must be that the historian, writing in banishment, and at a great distance of time, trusted to his imagination to supply the defect of his memory.'—LINGARD.

BAKER (SIR RICHARD).
—— Chronicle of the Kings of England. Third Edition, with a continuation by Edw. Philips. 1660.

BATE (G.), M.D.
Elenchi motuum nuperorum in Anglia. Pars Secunda: Simil ac Regis effugii mirabilis e Prœlio Wigorniæ enarratio. Authore Georgio Bateo, M.D. Regiæ Majestatis Proto-medico et Collegii Londinensis socio. Æræ Christianæ Anno 1662. Londini. Typis J. Flesher. Prostat Venalis apud R. Royston S. Regiæ Majestatis Bibliopolam. 1663. 8vo.
Reprinted 1676, 1685, etc.

JENINGS (A.).
Miraculum Basilicon; or, the Royale Miracle. Truly exhibiting the wonderful Preservation of his Sacred Majesty in, with his miraculous escape after, the Battel of Worcester; with his Deliverances at

Edgehill and in the Downs; faithfully collected and composed from the best and truest Relations; But as to that of Worcester, principally from the incomparable 'Elenchus motuum,' etc., as it was immediately delivered from the King's own mouth to the learned author. By A. J. Eirenophila-lethes. London. Printed in the year 1664.

Monarchy Revived in the most Illustrious Charles the Second, whose Life and Reign is exactly described in the ensuing Discourse. London. Printed by R. Daniel for Francis Eglesfield, at the Marygold, in St. Paul's Churchyard. MDCLX.

Dedicated to the happy Preserver of his Sacred Majesty, the Lady Jane Lane.

Reprinted in 1822. London, Charles Baldwyn.

The History of his Sacred Majesty Charles II., King of England, Scotland, France, and Ireland, Defender of the Faith, etc. Begun from the murder of his Royal Father of happy memory and continued to this present year 1660. By a person of quality. London. Printed for James Davies, and are to be sold at the Turk's head in Ivie Lane and at the Greyhound in St. Paul's Churchyard. 1660. 12mo, pp. xxii. + 236.

A copy of this small tract is in the British Museum.

England's Triumph, a more exact History of his Majestie's escape after the Battle of Worcester. London. 1660. 8vo.

> Mentioned in Lowndes''Bibliographers'Manual.'

The Five Faithful Brothers, a discourse between Charles II. and the five brothers at his escape from Worcester, with Mrs. Lane's conveying his Majesty through all his difficulties, etc. 1660. 12mo.

> Mentioned in Lowndes''Bibliographers'Manual.'

COLBORN (G.).

—— An exact narrative and relation of His Most Sacred Majesty's miraculous escape from Worcester on the third of September, 1651, till his arrival at Paris. Printed at London for G. Colborn. 1660. 4to, 8 pages.

> Reprinted in the Harleian Miscellany.

DANVERS, JOHN.

—— The Royal Oake; or, an historical description of the Royal Progress, wonderful travels, miraculous escapes of His Sacred Majesty Charles the Second, third Monarch of Great Brittain, etc. London. 1660. 4to.

> Reprinted in the Somers' 'Tracts.'

Whiteladies; or, His Sacred Majesty's most miraculous Preservation after the Battle at Worcester, September 3, 1651. Faithfully imparted for the satisfaction of the nation by eye-witnesses. By special command. London. Printed for the author, and are to be sold at the Royall Exchange and at Westminister. 1660. 12mo, pp. 39.

The copy of this small tract in the British Museum (Grenville Library) is believed to be unique. It is unfortunately imperfect.

Copy of a Letter written from a Prisoner at Chester, the $\frac{17}{27}$ September, and since Reviewed and Perfected by some on this side the sea, who were in the fight.

Printed in the Oxford Edition of Lord Clarendon's 'State Papers,' 1773; and by Hughes in the 'Boscobel Tracts.'

Whitgrave (T.) and Huddleston (J.).
—— A Summary of Occurrences relating to the miraculous Preservation of our late Sovereign Lord King Charles ii. after the defeat of his army at Worcester in the year 1651. Faithfully taken from the express Personal Testimony of those two worthy Roman Catholics, Thomas Whitgrave of Moseley in the County of Stafford, Esq., and Mr. John Huddleston, Priest of the Holy Order of St. Bennet, the eminent Instrument under God of the same Preservation. *Permissu Superiorum.* London. Printed by Henry Hills, Printer to the King's Most Excellent Majesty for his Household and Chappel; and are sold at his Printing-house on the Ditch Side in Black Friars. 1688. Pp. 34, 12mo.

WHITGRAVE (T.).

—— His account was first printed from the original MS. in an article in the *Retrospective Review*, vol. xiv. It was reprinted by Hughes, 'Boscobel Tracts,' 1830 and 1857.

MRS. ANNE WYNDHAM.

—— Claustrum Regale Reseratum; or, the King's Concealment at Trent. Published by A. W. London : Will Nott. 1667. 4to, pp. 48.

This pamphlet was reprinted with the Third Edition of 'Boscobel,' London, 1680, and with the Editions of 1709, 1725, and 1743. It is included in Hughes' 'Boscobel Tracts.'

LETTER of Mr. William Elledson (Ellison) to the Earl of Clarendon. From the Oxford Folio Edition of the Clarendon 'State Papers,' 1763. Reprinted in the 'Boscobel Tracts.'

CAPTAIN ALFORD'S NARRATIVE.

—— The original is in the Bodleian Library. It is printed in Cary's 'Memorials of the great Civil War.' London, 1842.

GOUNTER (GEORGE).

—— The last Act in the Miraculous Story of King Charles the Second's escape out of the reach of his tyrannical enemies, now first published from the original MS. London, 1846. 8vo.

—— Second Edition. London, 1873. 8vo.

The original of Colonel Gounter's narrative is in the Bodleian Library. It was printed in Cary's 'Memorials.'

BOSCOBEL

OR THE COMPLEAT HISTORY OF THE

MOST MIRACULOUS PRESERVATION OF

KING CHARLES THE SECOND

AFTER THE BATTLE OF WORCESTER

SEPTEMBER THE 3RD,

1651

KING'S MOST EXCELLENT MAJESTY

SIR,

Among the many addresses which every day offers your sacred majesty, this humbly hopes your particular gracious acceptance, since it has no other ambition than faithfully to represent to your majesty, and, by your royal permission, to all the world, the history of those miraculous providences that preserv'd you in the battle of Worcester, conceal'd you in the wilderness at Boscobel, and led you on your way towards a land where you might safely expect the returning favours of Heaven, which now, after so long a trial, has graciously heard our prayers, and abundantly crown'd your patience.

And, as in the conduct of a great part of this greatest affair, it pleased God (the more to endear his mercies) to make choice of many very little, though fit, instruments: so has my weakness, by this happy precedent, been encourag'd to hope it not unsuitable for me to relate what the wisest king thought proper for them to act; wherein yet I humbly beg your majesty's pardon, being conscious to myself of my utter incapacity to express, either your unparallel'd valour in the day of contending, or (which is a virtue far less usual for kings) your strong and even mind in the time of your sufferings.

From which sublime endowments of your most heroick majesty, I derive these comforts to myself, that whoever undertakes to reach at your perfections, must fall short as well as I, though not so much: And while I depend on your royal clemency more than others, I am more oblig'd to be

Your majesty's most loyal subject,

And most humble servant,

THO. BLOUNT.

TO THE READER

BEHOLD, I present you with an history of wonders; wonders so great, that, as no former age can parallel, succeeding times will scarce believe them.

Expect here to read the highest tyranny and rebellion that was ever acted by subjects, and the greatest hardships and persecutions that ever were suffered by a king; yet did his patience exceed his sorrows, and his virtue became at last victorious.

Some particulars, I confess, are so superlatively extraordinary, that I easily should fear they would scarce gain belief, even from my modern reader, had I not this strong argument to secure me, that no ingenuous person will think me so frontless, as knowingly to write an untruth in an history where his sacred majesty (my dread Sovereign, and the best of kings) bears the principal part, and most of the other persons concerned in the same action (except the Earl of Derby, Lord Wilmot, and Colonel Blague) still alive, ready to pour out shame and confusion on so impudent a forgery.

But I am so far from that foul crime of publishing what's false, that I can safely say I know not one line unauthentick; such has been my care to be sure of the truth, that I have diligently collected the particulars from most of their mouths, who were the very actors themselves in this scene of miracles.

To every individual person (as far as my industry could arrive to know) I have given the due of his merit, be it for valour, fidelity, or whatever other quality that any way had the honour to relate to his majesty's service.

In this later edition, I have added some particulars which came to my knowledge since the first publication; and have observed that, in this persecution, much of his majesty's actions and sufferings have run parallel with those of King David.

And though the whole complex may want elegance and politeness of style (which the nature of such relations does not properly challenge), yet it cannot want truth, the chief ingredient for such undertakings; in which assurance I am not afraid to venture myself in your hands.

Read on, and wonder !

BOSCOBEL

OR THE

HISTORY OF KING CHARLES THE SECOND'S MOST MIRACULOUS PRESERVATION AFTER THE BATTLE OF WORCESTER

PART I

IT was in June, in the year 1650, that Charles the Second, undoubted heir of Charles the First, of glorious memory, King of Great Britain, France, and Ireland (after his royal father had been barbarously murdered, and himself banished his own dominions, by his own rebellious subjects), took shipping at Scheveling, in Holland, and having escaped great dangers at sea, arrived soon after at Spey, in the north of Scotland.

On the first of January following, his majesty was crowned at Scoon, and an army raised in that kingdom to invade this, in hope to recover his regalities here, then most unjustly detained from him by some members of the Long Parliament, and Oliver Cromwell their general, who soon after most traitorously assumed the title of Protector of the new-minted commonwealth of England, Scotland, and Ireland.

Of this royal Scotch army the general officers were these: Lieutenant-General David Lesley, Lieutenant-General Middleton (who was since created Earl of Middleton, Lord Clarmont and Fettercairn), Major-General Massey, Major-General Montgomery, Major-General Daliel, and Major-General Vandrose, a Dutchman.

The first of August, 1651, his majesty, with his army began his march into England; and on the fifth of the same month, at his royal camp at Woodhouse, near the border, published his gracious declaration of general pardon and oblivion to all his loving subjects of the kingdom of England and dominion of Wales, that would desist from assisting the usurped authority of the pretended commonwealth of England, and return to the obedience they owed to their lawful king, and to the ancient happy government of the kingdom, except only

Oliver Cromwell, Henry Ireton, John Bradshaw, John Cook (pretended solicitor), and all others who did actually sit and vote in the murder of his royal father.

And lastly did declare, that the service being done, the Scotch army should quietly retire, that so all armies might be disbanded, and a lasting peace settled with religion and righteousness.

His majesty, after the publication of this gracious offer, marched his army into Lancashire, where he received some considerable supplies from the Earl of Derby (that loyal subject), and at Warrington Bridge met with the first opposition made by the rebels in England, but his presence soon put them to flight.

In this interim his majesty had sent a copy of his declaration, inclosed in a gracious letter to Thomas Andrews, then Lord Mayor (who had been one of his late majesty's judges), and the aldermen of the city of London, which, by order of the rump-rebels then sitting at Westminster, was (on the 26th of August) publickly burnt at the old Exchange by the hangman, and their own declaration proclaimed there and at Westminster, with beat of drum and sound of trumpet; by which his sacred majesty (to whom they could afford no better title than Charles Stuart), his abetters, agents, and complices, were declared traitors, rebels, and publick enemies. Impudence and treason beyond example!

After a tedious march of near three hundred miles, his majesty, with his army, on the 22nd of August, possessed himself of Worcester, after some small opposition made by the rebels there, commanded by Colonel John James. And at his entrance, the mayor of that city carried the sword before his majesty, who had left the Earl of Derby in Lancashire, as well to settle that and the adjacent countries in a posture of defence against Cromwell and his confederates, as to raise some auxiliary forces to recruit his majesty's army, in case the success of a battle should not prove so happy as all good men desired.

But (such was Heaven's decree) on the 25th of August, the earl's new rais'd forces, being overpowered, were totally defeated, near Wiggan, in that county, by Colonel Lilburn, with a regiment of rebellious sectaries. In which conflict the Lord Widdrington, Sir Thomas Tildesly, Colonel Trollop,

Colonel Bointon, Lieutenant-Colonel Galliard (faithful subjects and valiant soldiers), with some others of good note, were slain; Colonel Edward Roscarrock wounded; Sir William Throkmorton (since knight marshal to his majesty), Sir Timothy Fetherstonhaugh (who was beheaded by the rebels at Chester, on the 22nd of October following), Colonel Baines, and others, taken prisoners; and their general, the Earl of Derby (who charged the rebels valiantly, and received several wounds), put to flight with a small number of men: in which condition he made choice of the way towards Worcester, whither he knew his majesty's army was designed to march.

After some days, my lord, with Colonel Roscarrock and two servants, got into the confines of Staffordshire and Shropshire, near Newport, where at one Mr. Watson's house he met with Mr. Richard Snead (an honest gentleman of that county, and of his lordship's acquaintance), to whom he recounted the misfortune of his defeat at Wiggan, and the necessity of taking some rest, if Mr. Snead could recommend his lordship to any private house near hand, where he might safely continue till he could find an opportunity to go to his majesty.

Mr. Snead brought my lord and his company to
Boscobel House, a very obscure habitation, situate
in Shropshire, but adjoining upon Staffordshire, and
lies between Tong Castle and Brewood, in a kind of
wilderness.   John Giffard, Esq., who first built this
house, invited Sir Basil Brook, with other friends
and neighbours, to a housewarming feast; at which
time Sir Basil was desired by Mr. Giffard to give
the house a name, he aptly calls it BOSCOBEL (from
the Italian *Bosco-bello*, which in that language
signifies fair wood), because seated in the midst of
many fair woods.

At this place the earl arrived on the 29th of
August (being Friday), at night; but the house at
that time afforded no inhabitant except William
Penderel the housekeeper, and his wife, who, to
preserve so eminent a person, freely adventured to
receive my lord, and kept him in safety till Sunday
night following, when (according to my lord's desire
of going to Worcester) he conveyed him to Mr.
Humphrey Elliot's house, at Gataker Park (a true-
hearted royalist), which was about nine miles on
the way from Boscobel thither.   Mr. Elliot did
not only cheerfully entertain the earl, but lent him

ten pounds, and conducted him and his company safe to Worcester.

The next day after his majesty's arrival at Worcester, being Saturday the 23rd of August, he was proclaimed King of Great Britain, France, and Ireland, by Mr. Thomas Lisens, mayor, and Mr. James Bridges, sheriff, of that loyal city, with great acclamations.

On the same day his majesty published this following manifesto, or declaration :—

'Charles, by the grace of God, King of England, Scotland, France, and Ireland, Defender of the Faith, etc. To all whom it may concern, greeting. We desire not the effusion of blood, we covet not the spoil or forfeiture of our people; our declaration at our entry into this kingdom, the quiet behaviour and abstinence of our army throughout this long march, and our own general pardon declared to all the inhabitants of this city, without taking advantage of the opposition here made us, by a force of the enemy over-mastering them, until we have chased them away, have sufficiently certified both what we seek is only that the laws of England (which secure the right both of king and subject) may henceforth recover their due power and force, and all past bitterness of these unnatural wars be buried and forgotten. As a means whereunto, we have by our warrants of the date hereof, and do hereby summon, upon their allegiance, all the nobility, gentry, and others of what degree and condition soever, of our county of Worcester, from sixteen to sixty, to appear in their persons, and with any horses, arms, and ammunition they have or can procure, at Pitchcroft, near the city, on Tuesday next, being the 26th of this instant month, where our self will be present that day (and also the next, in case those of the further parts of the county shou'd not be able to come up sooner), to dispose of such of them as we shall think fit, for our service in the war, in defence of this city and county, and to add unto our marching army, and to apply others (therein versed) to matters of civil advice and government. Upon which appearance, we shall immediately declare to all present, and conforming themselves to our royal authority, our free pardon; not excluding from this summons, or the pardon held forth, or from trust and employment in our service, as we shall find them cordial

and useful therein, any person or persons heretofore, or at this time actually employed in opposition
to us, whether in the military way, as governours,
colonels, captains, common soldiers, or whatsoever
else; or in the civil, as sheriffs, under-sheriffs,
justices of the peace, collectors, high constables,
or any other higher or lower quality; for securing
of all whom before mentioned in their loyal addresses
and performances (besides our army [more than once
successful since our entrance] which will be between
them and the enemy, and the engagement of our
own person in their defence), we have directed this
city to be forthwith fortified, and shall use such
other helps and means as shall occur to us in order
to that end.   But, on the other side, if any person,
of what degree or quality soever, either through
disloyalty and disaffection, or out of fear of the
cruel usurpers and oppressors, accompanied with a
presumption upon our mercy and goodness, or lastly,
presuming upon any former service, shall oppose or
neglect us at this time, they shall find, that as we
have authority to punish in life, liberty, and estate,
so we want not now the power to do it, and (if
overmuch provoked) shall not want the will neither;

and in particular, unto those who have heretofore done and suffered for their loyalty, we say it is now in their hands either to double that score, or to strike it off; concluding with this, that although our disposition abound with tenderness to our people, yet we cannot think it such to let them lie under a confest slavery and false peace, when, as we well know, and all the world may see, we have force enough, with the conjunction of those that groan under the present yoak (we will not say to dispute, for that we shall do well enough with those we have brought with us), but clearly (without any considerable opposition) to restore, together with our self, the quiet, the liberty, and the laws of the English nation.

' Given at our City of Worcester, the 23rd of August, 1651, and in the third year of our reign.'

Upon Sunday the 24th of August, Mr. Crosby (an eminent divine of that city) preach'd before his majesty in the cathedral church, and in his prayer stiled his majesty, 'in all causes, and over all persons, next under God, supreme head and governour'; at which the presbyterian Scots took exception, and Mr. Crosby was afterwards admonished by some of them to forbear such expressions.

Tuesday the 26th of August was the rendezvous, in Pitchcroft, of such loyal subjects as came into his majesty's aid, in pursuance of his before-mentioned declaration and summons. Here appeared,—

Francis Lord Talbot, afterwards Earl of Shrewsbury, with about 60 horse.
Mr. Mervin Touchet, his lieut.-colonel.
Sir John Packington.
Sir Walter Blount.
Sir Ralph Clare.
Sir Rowland Berkley.
Sir John Winford.
Mr. Ralph Sheldon of Beoly.
Mr. John Washburn of Witchinford, with 40 horse.
Mr. Thos. Hornyold of Blackmore Park, with 40 horse.
Mr. William Seldon of Finstall.
Mr. Thomas Acton.
Captain Benbow.
Mr. Robert Blount of Kenswick.
Mr. Robert Wigmore of Lucton.
Mr. Edward Pennel the elder.
Captain Kingston.
Mr. Peter Blount.
Mr. Edward Blount.
Mr. Walter Walsh.
Mr. Charles Walsh.

Mr. William Dansey.

Mr. Francis Knotsford.

Mr. George Chambers, etc.

With divers others, who were honoured and encouraged by his majesty's presence. Notwithstanding which access, the number of his army, both
English and Scots, was conceived not to exceed
12,000 men—viz. 10,000 Scots, and about 2000
English; and those, too, not excellently armed, nor
plentifully stored with ammunition.

Meanwhile Cromwell (that grand patron of sectaries) has amass'd together a numerous body of
rebels, commanded by himself in chief, and by the
Lord Grey of Groby, Fleetwood, and Lambert, under
him, consisting of above 30,000 men (being generally the scum and froth of the whole kingdom),
one part of which were sectaries, who, through a
fanatick zeal, were become devotes to this great idol;
the other part seduc'd persons, who either by force
or fear were unfortunately made actors or partici-
pants in this so horrible and fatal a tragedy.

Thus, then, began the pickeerings to the grand
engagement, Major-General Massey, with a commanded party, being sent by his majesty to secure

the bridge and pass at Upton, upon Severn, seven miles below Worcester. On Thursday the 28th of August, Lambert with a far greater number of rebels attacked him, and after some dispute gained the pass, the river being then fordable. Yet the major-general behav'd himself very gallantly, received a shot in the hand from some musketiers the enemy had conveyed into the church, and retreated in good order to Worcester.

During this encounter, Cromwell himself (whose head-quarter was the night before at Pershore) advanced to Stoughton, within four miles of the city, on the south side, himself quartered that night at Mr. Simon's house, at White Lady-Aston; and a party of his horse faced the city that evening.

The next day (August the 29th) Sultan Oliver appeared with a great body of horse and foot on Red Hill, within a mile of Worcester, where he made a bonnemine, but attempted nothing; and that night part of his army quartered at Judge Barkley's house at Speachley. The same day it was resolved by his majesty, at a council of war, to give the grand rebel a camisado, by beating up his quarters that night with 1500 select horse and foot, commanded by Lieut.-General Middleton and Sir William Keyth, all of them wearing their shirts over their armour for distinction; which accordingly was attempted and might in all probability have been successful, had not the design been most traiterously discovered to the rebels by one Guyse, a tailor in the town, and a notorious sectary, who was hanged the day following, as the just reward of his treachery. In this action Major Knox was slain, and some few taken prisoners by the enemy. A considerable party of the rebels, commanded by Colonel Fleetwood, Colonel Richard Ingoldsby (who since became a real convert, and was created Knight of the Bath at his majesty's coronation), Colonel Goff, and Colonel Gibbons, being got over the Severn, at Upton, marched next day to Powick-town, when they made an halt; for Powick-bridge (lying upon the river Team, between Powick-town and Worcester) was guarded by a brigade of his majesty's horse and foot, commanded by Major-General Robert Montgomery and Colonel George Keyth.

The fatal 3rd of September being come, his majesty this day (holding a council of war upon the top of the college church steeple, the better to discover the enemies' posture) observed some firing at Powick, and Cromwell making a bridge of boats over Severn, under Bunshill, about a mile below the city towards Team-mouth; his majesty presently goes down, commands all to their arms, and marches in person to Powick-bridge, to give orders, as well for maintaining that bridge, as for opposing the making the other of boats, and hastened back to his army in the city.

Soon after his majesty was gone from Powick-bridge, the enemy assaulted it furiously, which was well defended by Montgomery, till himself was dangerously wounded and his ammunition spent, so that he was forced to make a disorderly retreat into Worcester, leaving Collonel Keyth a prisoner at the bridge. At the same time Cromwell had with much celerity finish'd his bridge of boats and planks over the main river, without any considerable opposition, saving that Colonel Pitscotty, with about three hundred Highlanders, performed as much therein as could be expected from a handful of men fighting against great numbers. By this means Oliver held communication with those of his party at

Powick-bridge, and when he had marched over a considerable number of his men, said (in his hypocritical way), 'The Lord of Hosts be with you'; and return'd himself to raise a battery of great guns against the fort royal on the south side of the city.

His majesty being return'd from Powick-bridge, march'd with the Duke of Buckingham, Lord Grandison, and some of his cavalry, through the city, and out at Sudbury-gate by the fort royal, where the rebels' great shot came frequently near his sacred person.

At this time Cromwell was settled in an advantageous post at Perrywood, within a mile of the city, swelling with pride, and confident in the numbers of his men, having besides rais'd a breastwork, at the cockshoot of that wood, for his greater security; but Duke Hamilton (formerly Lord Lanerick), with his own troop and some Highlanders, Sir Alexander Forbes, with his regiment of foot, and divers English lords and gentlemen voluntiers, by his majesty's command and encouragement, engaged him, and did great execution upon his best men, forced the great sultan (as the Rhodians in like case did the Turk) to retreat with his janizaries;

and his majesty was once as absolute master of his great guns as he ought then to have been of the whole land.

Here his majesty gave an incomparable example of valour to the rest, by charging in person, which the Highlanders, especially, imitated in a great measure, fighting with the but-end of their muskets when their ammunition was spent; but new supplies of rebels being continually poured upon them, and the main body of Scotch horse not coming up in due time from the town to his majesty's relief, his army was forced to retreat in at Sudbury-gate in much disorder.

In this action Duke Hamilton (who fought valiantly) had his horse killed under him, and was himself mortally wounded, of which he died within few days, and many of his troop (consisting much of gentlemen, and diverse of his own name) were slain; Sir John Douglas received his death's wound; and Sir Alex. Forbes (who was the first knight the king made in Scotland, and commanded the fort royal here) was shot through both the calves of his legs, lay in the wood all night, and was brought prisoner to Worcester next day.

The rebels in this encounter had great advantage, as well in their numbers, as by fighting both with horse and foot against his majesty's foot only, the greatest part of his horse being wedged up in the town. And when the foot were defeated, a part of his majesty's horse fought afterwards against both the enemy's horse and foot upon great disadvantage. And as they had few persons of condition among them to lose, so no rebels, but Quartermaster-general Mosely and one Captain Jones, were worth taking notice of to be slain in this battle.

At Sudbury-gate (I know not whether by accident or on purpose) a cart laden with ammunition was overthrown and lay across the passage, one of the oxen that drew it being there killed; so that his majesty could not ride into the town, but was forced to dismount and come in on foot.

The rebels soon after stormed the fort royal (the fortifications whereof were not perfected), and put all the Scots they found therein to the sword.

In the Friars-street his majesty put off his armour, (which was heavy and troublesome to him), and took a fresh horse; and then perceiving many of his foot soldiers began to throw down their arms and decline fighting, he rode up and down among them, sometimes with his hat in his hand, entreating them to stand to their arms and fight like men, other whiles encouraging them, alleging the goodness and justice of the cause they fought for ; but seeing himself not able to prevail, said, 'I had rather you would shoot me, than keep me alive to see the sad consequences of this fatal day.' So deep a sense had his prophetic soul of the miseries of his beloved country, even in the midst of his own danger.

During this hot engagement at Perrywood and Redhill, the rebels on the other side the water possessed themselves of St. John's ; and a brigade of his majesty's foot which were there, under the command of Major-General Daliel, without any great resistance, laid down their arms and craved quarter.

When some of the enemy were entered, and entering the town both at the Key, Castle-hill, and Sudbury-gate, without any conditions, the Earl of Cleveland, Sir James Hamilton, Colonel Thomas Wogan, Colonel William Carlis (then major to the Lord Talbot), Lieut.-Colonel John Slaughter,

Captain Thos. Hornyold, Captain Thos. Giffard, Captain John Astley, Mr. Peter Blount, and Captain Richard Kemble (captain-lieutenant to the Lord Talbot), and some others, rallied what force they could (though inconsiderable to the rebels' numbers), and charged the enemy very gallantly both in Sudbury-street and High-street, where Sir James and Captain Kemble were desperately wounded, and others slain; yet this action did much secure his majesty's march out at St. Martin's-gate, who had otherwise been in danger of being taken in the town.

About the same time, the Earl of Rothes, Sir William Hamilton, and Colonel Drummond, with a party of Scots, maintained the Castle-hill with much resolution, till such time as conditions were agreed on for quarter.

Lastly, some of his majesty's English army valiantly opposed the rebels at the Town-hall, where Mr. Coningsby Colles and some others were slain; Mr. John Rumney, Mr. Chas. Wells, and others, taken prisoners; so that the rebels having in the end subdued all their opponents, fell to plundering the city unmercifully, few or none of the citizens escaping but such as were of the fanatick party.

When his majesty saw no hope of rallying his thus discomfited foot, he marched out of Worcester, at St. Martin's-gate (the Fore-gate being mured up), about six of the clock in the evening, with his main body of horse, as then commanded by General David Lesley, but were now in some confusion.

The Lord St. Clare, with diverse of the Scottish nobility and gentry, were taken prisoners in the town ; and the foot soldiers (consisting most of Scots) were almost all either slain or taken, and such of them who in the battle escaped death lived but longer to die, for the most part, more miserably, many of them being afterwards knocked o' the head by country people, some bought and sold like slaves, for a small price, others went begging up and down, till, charity failing them, their necessities brought upon them diseases, and diseases death.

Before his majesty was come to Barbon's-bridge, about half a mile out of Worcester, he made several stands, faced about, and desired the Duke of Buckingham, Lord Wilmot, and other of his commanders, that they might rally and try the fortune

of war once more. But at the bridge a serious
consultation was held; and then perceiving many
of the troopers to throw off their arms and
shift for themselves, they were all of opinion the
day was irrecoverably lost, and that their only
remaining work was to save the king from those
ravenous wolves and regicides. Whereupon his
majesty, by advice of his council, resolved to march
with all speed for Scotland, following therein the
steps of King David, his great predecessor in royal
patience, who, finding himself in circumstances not
unlike to these, ' said unto all his servants that were
with him at Jerusalem, Arise, and let us flee; for we
shall not else escape from Absalom : make speed to
depart, lest he overtake us suddenly, and bring evil
upon us, and smite the city with the edge of the
sword.'

Immediately after this result, the duke asked the
Lord Talbot (being of that country) if he could
direct the way northwards. His lordship answered,
that he had one Richard Walker in his troop
(formerly a scout-master in those parts, and who
since died in Jamaica) that knew the way well,
who was accordingly called to be the guide, and

performed that duty for some miles ; but being
come to Kinver-heath, not far from Kederminster,
and daylight being gone, Walker was at a puzzle in
the way.

Here his majesty made a stand, and consulted
with the duke, Earl of Derby, Lord Wilmot, etc.,
to what place he might march, at least to take
some hour's rest.   The Earl of Derby told his
majesty, that in his flight from Wiggan to Worcester
he had met with a perfect honest man, and a great
convenience of concealment at Boscobel House
(before mentioned), but withal acquainted the king
it was a recusant's house ; and it was suggested, that
those people (being accustomed to persecution and
searches) were most like to have the readiest means
and safest contrivances to preserve him : his majesty
therefore inclined to go thither.

The Lord Talbot being made acquainted therewith, and finding Walker dubious of the way, called
for Mr. Charles Giffard (a faithful subject, and of
the ancient family of Chillington) to be his majesty's
conductor, which office Mr. Giffard willingly undertook, having one Yates a servant with him, very
expert in the ways of that country ; and being

come near Sturbridge, it was under consideration whether his majesty should march through that town or no, and resolved in the affirmative, and that all about his person should speak French, to prevent any discovery of his majesty's presence.

Meantime General Lesley, with the Scottish horse, had, in the close of the evening, taken the more direct way northward, by Newport, his majesty being left only attended by the Duke of Buckingham, Earl of Derby, Earl of Lauderdale, Lord Talbot, Lord Wilmot, Colonel Thomas Blague, Colonel Edward Roscarrock, Mr. Marmaduke Darcy, Mr. Richard Lane, Mr. William Armorer (since knighted), Mr. Hugh May, Mr. Charles Giffard, Mr. Peter Street, and some others, in all about sixty horse.

At a house about a mile beyond Sturbridge, his majesty drank and ate a crust of bread, the house affording no better provision; and as his majesty rode on, he discoursed with Colonel Roscarrock touching Boscobel House, and the means of security which the Earl of Derby and he found at that place.

However, Mr. Giffard humbly proposed to carry

his majesty first to White Ladies (another seat of the Giffards), lying but half a mile beyond Boscobel, where he might repose himself for a while, and then take such farther resolution as his majesty and council should think fit.

This house is distant about twenty-six miles from Worcester, and still retains the ancient name of White Ladies, from its having formerly been a monastery of Cistertian nuns, whose habit was of that colour.

His majesty and his retinue (being safely conducted thither by Mr. Giffard) alighted, now, as they hoped, out of danger of any present surprise by pursuits; George Penderel (who was a servant in the house) opened the doors; and after his majesty and the lords were entered the house, his majesty's horse was brought into the hall, and by this time it was about break of day on Thursday morning. Here every one was in a sad consult how to escape the fury of bloodthirsty enemies; but the greatest solicitude was to save the king, who was both hungry and tired with this long and hasty march.

Mr. Giffard presently sent for Richard Penderel,

who lived near hand at Hobbal Grange; and
Colonel Roscarrock caused Bartholomew Martin, a
boy in the house, to be sent to Boscobel for William
Penderel; meantime Mrs. Giffard brought his
majesty some sack and biscuit; for 'the king, and
all the people that were with him, came weary, and
refreshed themselves there.' Richard came first,
and was immediately sent back to bring a suit of
his clothes for the king; and by that time he
arrived with them, William came, and both were
brought into the parlour to the Earl of Derby, who
immediately carried them into an inner parlour
(where the king was), and told William Penderel,
'This is the king,' pointing to his majesty; 'thou
must have a care of him, and preserve him as thou
didst me.' And Mr. Giffard did also much conjure
Richard to have a special care of his charge; to
which commands the two brothers yielded ready
obedience.

Whilst Richard and William were thus sent for,
his majesty had been advised to rub his hands on
the back of the chimney, and with them his face,
for a disguise, and some person had disorderly cut
off his hair. His majesty having put off his garter,

blue riband, George of diamonds, buff-coat, and other princely ornaments, committed his watch to the custody of the Lord Wilmot, and his George to Colonel Blague, and distributed the gold he had in his pocket among his servants, and then put on a noggen coarse shirt, which was borrowed of Edward Martin, who lived in the house, and Richard Penderel's green suit and leather doublet, but had not time to be so disguised as he was afterwards, for both William and Richard Penderel did advertise the company to make haste away, in regard there was a troop of rebels commanded by Colonel Ashenhurst, quartered at Cotsal, but three miles distant, some of which troop came to the house within half an hour after the dissolution of the royal troop. 'Thus David and his men departed out of Keilah, and went whithersoever they could go.'

Richard Penderel conducted the king out at a back door, unknown to most of the company (except some of the lords, and Colonel Roscarrock, who, with sad hearts, but hearty prayers, took leave of him), and carried him into an adjacent wood belonging to Boscobel, called Spring Coppice, about half a mile from White Ladies (where he abode, as

David did in the wilderness of Ziph, 'in a wood,') whilst William, Humphrey, and George, were scouting abroad to bring what news they could learn to his majesty in the coppice, as occasion required.

His majesty being thus, as they hoped, in a way of security, the duke, Earl of Derby, Earl of Lauderdale, Lord Talbot, and the rest (having Mr. Giffard for their guide, and being then not above forty horse, of which number his majesty's pad-nag was one, ridden by Mr. Richard Lane, one of the grooms of the bed-chamber), marched from White Ladies northwards by the way of Newport, in hope to overtake or meet General Lesley with the main body of Scotch horse.

As soon as they were got into the road, the Lord Leviston (who commanded his majesty's life guard) overtook them, pursued by a party of rebels under the command of Colonel Blundel: the lords with their followers faced about, fought, and repelled them; but when they came a little beyond Newport, some of Colonel Lilburn's men met them in the front, other rebels, from Worcester, pursued in the rear; themselves and horses being sufficiently tired,

the Earl of Derby, Earl of Lauderdale, Mr. Charles
Giffard, and some others, were taken and carried
prisoners, first to Whitchurch, and from thence to
an inn in Bunbury, in Cheshire, where Mr. Giffard
found means to make an escape; but the noble
Earl of Derby was thence conveyed to Westchester,
and there tried by a pretended court-martial, held
the 1st of October 1651, by virtue of a commission
from Cromwell, grounded on an execrable rump-act,
of the 12th of August, then last past, the very title
whereof cannot be mentioned without horror; but it
pretended most traitorously to prohibit correspondence with Charles Stuart (their lawful sovereign),
under penalty of high treason, loss of life and
estate,—Prodigious rebels !

In this Black Tribunal there sate, as Judges, these Persons,
and under these titles :

Colonel Humphrey Mackworth, president.
Major-General Mitton.
Colonel Robert Duckenfield.
Colonel Henry Bradshaw.
Colonel Thomas Croxton.
Colonel George Twisleton.
Lieutenant-Colonel Henry Birkenhead.
Lieutenant-Colonel Simon Finch.

Lieutenant-Colonel Alexander Newton.
Captain James Stepford.
Captain Samuel Smith.
Captain John Downes.
Captain Vincent Corbet.
Captain John Delves.
Captain John Griffith.
Captain Thomas Portington.
Captain Edward Alcock.
Captain Ralph Pownall.
Captain Richard Grantham.
Captain Edward Stelfax.

THEIR CRUEL SENTENCE.

'*Resolved by the Court upon the question:* That James, Earl of Derby, is guilty of the breach of the Act of the 12th of August 1651, last past, entituled, "An Act prohibiting Correspondence with Charles Stuart or his Party," and so of high treason against the commonwealth of England, and is therefore worthy of death.

'*Resolved by the Court:* That the said James, Earl of Derby, is a traitor to the commonwealth of England, and an abetter, encourager, and assister of the declared traitors and enemies thereof, and shall be put to death by severing his head from his body, at the market-place in the town of Bolton, in Lancashire, upon Wednesday the 15th day of this instant October, about the hour of one of the clock the same day.'

This was the authority, and some of these the persons, that so barbarously, and contrary to the law of nations, condemned this noble earl to death, notwithstanding his just plea, 'That he had quarter for life given him by one Captain Edge, who took him prisoner.' But this could not obtain justice, nor any intercession, mercy; so that on the 15th of the said October he was accordingly beheaded at Bolton in a most barbarous and inhumane manner.

The Earl of Lauderdale, with several others, were carried prisoners to the Tower, and afterwards to Windsor Castle, where they continued divers years.

Whilst the rebels were plundering those noble persons, the duke, with the Lord Leviston, Colonel Blague, Mr. Marmaduke Darcy, and Mr. Hugh May, forsook the road first, and soon after their horses, and betook themselves to a by-way, and got into Bloore Park, near Cheswardine, about five miles from Newport, where they received some refresh-

ment at a little obscure house of Mr. George
Barlow's, and afterwards met with two honest
labourers, in an adjoining wood, to whom they
communicated the exigent and distress which the
fortune of war had reduced them to; and finding
them like to prove faithful, the duke thought fit
to imitate his royal master, delivered his George
(which was given him by the Queen of England)
to Mr. May (who preserved it through all difficulties, and afterwards restored it to his grace in
Holland), and changed habit with one of the
workmen; and in this disguise, by the assistance
of Mr. Barlow and his wife, was, after some days,
conveyed by one Nicholas Matthews, a carpenter,
to the house of Mr. Hawley, an hearty cavalier, at
Bilstrop, in Nottinghamshire, from thence to the
Lady Villiars' house at Booksby, in Leicestershire;
and after many hardships and encounters, his grace
got secure to London, and from thence to his
majesty in France.

At the same time the Lord Leviston, Colonel
Blague, Mr. Darcy, and Mr. May, all quitted their
horses, disguised themselves, and severally shifted
for themselves, and some of them, through various

dangers and sufferings, contrived their escapes; in particular, Mr. May was forced to lie twenty-one days in a hay-mow belonging to one John Bold an honest husbandman, who lived at Soudley: Bold having all that time rebel soldiers quartered in his house, yet failed not to give a constant relief to his more welcome guest; and when the coast was clear of soldiers, Mr. May came to London on foot in his disguise.

The Lord Talbot (seeing no hope of rallying) hasted towards his father's house at Longford, near Newport; where being arrived, he conveyed his horse into a neighbouring barn, but was immediately pursued by the rebels, who found the horse saddled, and by that concluded my lord not to be far off, so that they searched Longford House narrowly, and some of them continued in it four or five days, during all which time my lord was in a close place in one of the out-houses, almost stifled for want of air, and had perished for want of food, had he not been once relieved in the dead of the night, and with much difficulty, by a trusty servant; yet his lordship thought it a great providence, even by these hardships, to escape the fury of such enemies, who sought the destruction of the nobility, as well as of their king.

In this interim the valiant Earl of Cleveland (who, being above sixty years of age, had marched twenty-one days together upon a trotting-horse) had also made his escape from Worcester, when all the fighting work was over, and was got to Woodcot, in Shropshire, whither he was pursued, and taken at or near Mistress Broughton's house, from whence he was carried prisoner to Stafford, and from thence to the Tower of London.

Colonel Blague, remaining at Mr. Barlow's house at Bloor-pipe, about eight miles from Stafford, his first action was, with Mistress Barlow's privity and advice, to hide his majesty's George under a heap of chips and dust; yet the colonel could not conceal himself so well, but that he was here, soon after, taken and carried prisoner to Stafford, and from thence conveyed to the Tower of London. Meantime the George was transmitted to Mr. Robert Milward, of Stafford, for better security, who afterwards faithfully conveyed it to Colonel Blague in the Tower, by the trusty hands of Mr. Isaac Walton; and the Colonel not long after happily escaping thence, restored it to his majesty's own hands, which had been thus wonderfully preserved from being made a prize to sordid rebels.

The Scotch cavalry (having no place to retreat unto nearer than Scotland) were soon after dispersed, and most of them taken by the rebels and country people in Cheshire, Lancashire, and parts adjacent.

Thus was this royal army totally subdued, thus dispersed; and if in this so important an affair, any of the Scottish commanders were treacherous at Worcester (as some suspected), he has a great account to make for the many years' miseries that ensued thereby to both nations, under the tyrannical, usurped government of Cromwell.

But to return to the duty of my attendance on his sacred majesty in Spring Coppice. By that time Richard Penderel had conveyed him into the obscurest part of it, it was about sun-rising on Thursday morning, and the heavens wept bitterly at these calamities, insomuch as the thickest tree in the wood was not able to keep his majesty dry, nor was there anything for him to sit on; wherefore Richard went to Francis Yates' house (a trusty neighbour, who married his wife's sister), where he borrowed a blanket, which he folded and laid on the ground under a tree for his majesty to sit on.

At the same time Richard spoke to the good-wife Yates to provide some victuals, and bring it into the wood at a place he appointed her. She presently made ready a mess of milk, and some butter and eggs, and brought them to his majesty in the wood, who, being a little surprised to see the woman (no good concealer of a secret), said cheerfully to her, 'Good woman, can you be faithful to a distressed cavalier?' She answered, 'Yes, sir, I will rather die than discover you.' With which answer his majesty was well satisfied, and received from her hands, as David did from Abigail's, 'that which she brought him.'

The Lord Wilmot in the interim took John Penderel for his guide, but knew not determinately whither to go, purposing at first to have marched northwards; but as they passed by Brewood forge, the forgemen made after them, till being told by one Rich. Dutton that it was Colonel Crompton whom they pursued, the Vulcans happily, upon that mistake, quitted the chase.

Soon after they narrowly escaped a party of
rebels as they passed by Covenbrook; so that
seeing danger on every side, and John meeting with
William Walker (a trusty neighbour), committed my
lord to his care and counsel, who for the present
conveyed them into a dry marl pit, where they
stayed a while, and afterwards to one Mr. Huntbache's house at Brinsford, and put their horses into
John Evan's barn, whilst John Penderel goes to
Wolverhampton to see what convenience he could
find for my lord's coming thither, but met with
none, the town being full of soldiers.

Yet John leaves no means unessayed, hastens to
Northcot (an adjacent village), and there, whilst he
was talking with good-wife Underhill (a neighbour),
in the instant Mr. John Huddleston (a sojourner
at Mr. Thomas Whitgreave's of Moseley, and of
John's acquaintance) was accidentally passing by, to
whom John (well assured of his integrity) presently
addresses himself and his business, relates to him
the sad news of the defeat of his majesty's army at
Worcester, and discovers in what strait and confusion he had left his majesty and his followers at
White Ladies, and in particular, that he had

brought thence a person of quality (for John then knew not who my lord was) to Huntbache's house, who, without present relief, would be in great danger of being taken.

Mr. Huddleston goes home forthwith, takes John with him, and acquaints Mr. Whitgreave with the business, who freely resolved to venture all, rather than such a person should miscarry.

Hereupon Mr. Whitgreave repairs to Huntbache's house, speaks with my lord, and gives direction how he should be privately conveyed into his house at Moseley, about ten of the clock at night; and though it so fell out that the directions were not punctually observed, yet my lord and his man were at last brought into the house, where Mr. Whitgreave (after some refreshment given them) conveys them into a secret place, which my lord admiring for its excellent contrivance, and solicitous for his majesty's safety, said, ' I would give a world my friend,' meaning the king, ' were here'; and then (being abundantly satisfied of Mr. Whitgreave's fidelity) deposited in his hands a little bag of jewels, which my lord received again at his departure.

As soon as it was day, Mr. Whitgreave sent

William Walker with my lord's horses to his neighbour, Colonel John Lane of Bentley, near Walsall, south-east from Moseley about four miles (whom Mr. Whitgreave knew to be a right honest gentleman, and ready to contribute any assistance to so charitable a work), and wished Walker to acquaint the colonel that they belonged to some eminent person about the king, whom he could better secure than the horses. The colonel willingly receives them, and sends word to Mr. Whitgreave to meet him that night in a close not far from Moseley, in order to the tender of farther service to the owner of the horses, whose name neither the colonel nor Mr. Whitgreave yet knew.

On Thursday night when it grew dark, his majesty resolved to go from those parts into Wales, and to take Richard Penderel with him for his guide; but, before they began their journey, his majesty went into Richard's house at Hobbal Grange, where the old good-wife Penderel had not only the honour to see his majesty, but to see him attended by her son Richard. Here his majesty had time and means better to complete his disguise. His name was agreed to be Will. Jones, and his arms a wood-bill. In this posture, about nine o'clock at night (after some refreshment taken in the house), his majesty, with his trusty servant Richard, began their journey on foot, resolving to go that night to Madeley, in Shropshire, about five miles from White Ladies, and within a mile of the river Severn, over which their way lay for Wales. In this village lived one Mr. Francis Woolf, an honest gentleman of Richard's acquaintance.

His majesty had not been long gone, but the Lord Wilmot sent John Penderel from Mr. Whitgreave's to White Ladies and Boscobel, to know in what security the king was. John returned and acquainted my lord that his majesty was marched from thence. Hereupon my lord began to consider which way himself should remove with safety.

Colonel Lane, having secured my lord's horses, and being come to Moseley, according to appointment, on Friday night, was brought up to my lord by Mr. Whitgreave, and (after mutual salutation) acquainted him that his sister, Mrs. Jane Lane, had by accident procured a pass from some commander of the rebels, for herself and a man to go a little

beyond Bristol, to see Mrs. Norton, her special
friend, then near her time of lying in, and freely
offered, if his lordship thought fit, he might make
use of it; which my lord seemed inclinable to
accept, and on Saturday night was conducted by
Colonel Lane's man (himself not being well) to
the Colonel's house at Bentley; his lordship then,
and not before, discovering his name to Mr.
Whitgreave, and giving him many thanks for so
great a kindness in so imminent a danger.

Before his majesty came to Madeley, he met
with an ill-favoured encounter at Evelin Mill, being
about two miles from thence. The miller (it seems)
was an honest man, but his majesty and Richard
knew it not, and had then in his house some considerable persons of his majesty's army, who took
shelter there in their flight from Worcester, and
had not been long in the mill, so that the miller
was upon his watch; and Richard unhappily per-
mitting a gate to clap, through which they passed,
gave occasion to the miller to come out of the mill
and boldly ask, 'Who is there?' Richard, thinking
the miller had pursued them, quitted the usual way
in some haste, and led his majesty over a little

brook, which they were forced to wade through, and which contributed much towards the galling his majesty's feet, who (as he afterwards pleasantly observed) was here in some danger of losing his guide, but that the rustling of Richard's calves-skin breeches was the best direction his majesty had to follow him in that dark night.

They arrived at Madeley about midnight ; Richard goes to Mr. Woolf's house, where they were all in bed, knocks them up, and acquaints Mr. Woolf's daughter (who came to the door) that the king was there, who presently received him into the house, where his majesty refreshed himself for some time ; but understanding the rebels kept several guards upon Severn, and it being feared that some of their party (of which many frequently passed through the town) might quarter at the house (as had often happened), it was apprehended unsafe for his majesty to lodge in the house (which afforded no secret place for concealment), but rather to retire into a barn near adjoining, as less liable to the danger of a surprise; whither his majesty went accordingly, and continued in a hay-mow there all the day following his servant Richard attending him.

During his majesty's stay in the barn, Mr Woolf
had often conference with him about his intended
journey, and in order thereto took care, by a trusty
servant (sent abroad for that purpose), to inform
himself more particularly of those guards upon
Severn, and had certain word brought him, that not
only the bridges were secured, but all the passage-
boats seized on, insomuch that he conceived it very
hazardous for his majesty to prosecute his design
for Wales, but rather go to Boscobel House, being the
most retired place for concealment in all the country,
and to stay there till an opportunity of a farther
safe conveyance could be found out; which advice
his majesty inclined to approve, and thereupon resolved for Boscobel the night following.   In the
meantime, his hands not appearing sufficiently dis-
coloured, suitable to his other disguise, Mrs Woolf
provided walnut-tree leaves as the readiest expedient
for that purpose.

The day being over, his majesty adventured to
come again into the house, where having for some
time refreshed himself, and being furnished with
conveniences for his journey (which was conceived
to be safer on foot than by horse), he with his

faithful guide Richard, about eleven o'clock at night, set forth toward Boscobel.

About three of the clock on Saturday morning, being come near the house, Richard left his majesty in the wood, whilst he went in to see if any soldiers were there, or other danger ; where he found Colonel William Carlis (who had seen, not the last man born, but the last man killed, at Worcester, and) who, having with much difficulty made his escape from thence, was got into his own neighbourhood, and for some time concealing himself in Boscobel Wood, was come that morning to the house to get some relief of William Penderel, his old acquaintance.

Richard having acquainted the colonel that the king was in the wood, the colonel, with William and Richard, went presently thither to give their attendance, where they found his majesty sitting on the root of a tree, who was glad to see the colonel, and came with them into the house, where he eat bread and cheese heartily, and (as an extraordinary) William Penderel's wife made his majesty a posset of thin milk and small beer, and got ready some warm water to wash his feet, not only extreme dirty, but much galled with travel.

The colonel pulled off his majesty's shoes, which were full of gravel, and stockings, which were very wet; and there being no other shoes in the house that would fit him, the good-wife put some hot embers in those to dry them, whilst his majesty's feet were washing and his stockings shifted.

Being thus a little refreshed, the colonel persuaded his majesty to go back into the wood (supposing it safer than the house), where the colonel made choice of a thick-leaved oak, into which William and Richard helped them both up, and brought them such provision as they could get, with a cushion for his majesty to sit on; the colonel humbly desired his majesty (who had taken little or no rest the two preceding nights) to seat himself as easily as he could in the tree, and rest his head on the colonel's lap, who was watchful that his majesty might not fall. In this oak they continued most part of the day; and in that posture his majesty slumbered away some part of the time, and bore all these hardships and afflictions with incomparable patience.

In the evening they returned to the house, where William Penderel acquainted his majesty with the secret place wherein the Earl of Derby had been

secured, which his majesty liked so well, that he resolved, whilst he stayed there, to trust only to that,
and go no more into the royal oak, as from hence it
must be called, where he could not so much as sit at
ease.

His majesty now finding himself in a hopeful
security, permitted William Penderel to shave him,
and cut the hair off his head as short at top as the
scissors would do it, but leaving some about the ears,
according to the country mode; Colonel Carlis attending, told his majesty, 'William was but a mean
barber'; to which his majesty answered, 'He had
never been shaved by any barber before.' The king
bade William burn the hair which he cut off; but
William was only disobedient in that, for he kept a
good part of it, wherewith he has since pleasured
some persons of honour, and is kept as a civil
relic.

Humphrey Penderel was this Saturday designed
to go to Shefnal, to pay some taxes to one Captain
Broadway; at whose house he met with a colonel of
the rebels, who was newly come from Worcester in
pursuit of the king, and who, being informed that
his majesty had been at White Ladies, and that

Humphrey was a near neighbour to the place, exa-
mined him strictly, and laid before him, as well the
penalty for concealing the king, which was death
without mercy, as the reward for discovering him,
which should be one thousand pounds certain pay.
But neither fear of punishment, nor hope of reward,
was able to tempt Humphrey into any disloyalty ;
he pleaded ignorance, and was dismissed, and on
Saturday night related to his majesty and the loyal
colonel at Boscobel what had passed betwixt him
and the rebel colonel at Shefnal.

This night the good-wife (whom his majesty was
pleased to call 'my dame Joan') provided some
chickens for his majesty's supper (a dainty he had
not lately been acquainted with), and a little pallet
was put into the secret place for his majesty to
rest in; some of the brothers being continually
upon duty, watching the avenues of the house and
the roadway, to prevent the danger of a surprise.

After supper Colonel Carlis asked his majesty
what meat he would please to have provided for
the morrow, being Sunday; his majesty desired
some mutton, if it might be had.   But it was
thought dangerous for William to go to any market

to buy it, since his neighbours all knew he did not use to buy such for his own diet, and so it might beget a suspicion of his having strangers at his house.   But the colonel found another expedient to satisfy his majesty's desires.   Early on Sunday morning he repairs to Mr. Wm. Staunton's sheep-coat, who rented some of the demeans of Boscobel; here he chose one of the best sheep, sticks him with his dagger, then sends William for the mutton, who brings him home on his back.

On Sunday morning (September the 7th) his majesty got up early, his dormitory being none of the best, nor his bed the easiest, and, near the secret place where he lay, had the convenience of a gallery to walk in, where he was observed to spend some time in his devotions, and where he had the advantage of a window, which surveyed the road from Tong to Brewood.   Soon after his majesty coming down into the parlour, his nose fell a-bleeding, which put his poor faithful servants into a great fright; but his majesty was pleased soon to remove it by telling them it often did so.

As soon as the mutton was cold, William cut it up and brought a leg of it into the parlour; his majesty called for a knife and a trencher, and cut some of it into collops, and pricked them with the knife point, then called for a frying-pan and butter, and fried the collops himself, of which he eat heartily ; Colonel Carlis the while being but under cook, and that honour enough too, made the fire and turned the collops in the pan.

When the colonel afterwards attended his majesty in France, his majesty calling to remembrance this passage among others, was pleased merrily to propose it, as a problematical question, whether himself or the colonel were the master-cook at Boscobel, and the supremacy was of right adjudged to his majesty.

All this while the other brothers of the Penderels were, in their several stations, either scouting abroad to learn intelligence, or upon some other service ; but it so pleased God, that, though the soldiers had some intelligence of his majesty's having been at White Ladies, and none that he was gone thence, yet this house (which proved a happy sanctuary for his majesty in his sad exigent) had not at all been searched during his Majesty's abode there, though that had several times ; this, perhaps, the rather escaping, because the neighbours could truly inform none but poor servants lived here.

His majesty spent some part of this Lord's day in reading, in a pretty arbour in Boscobel garden, which grew upon a mount, and wherein there was a stone table, and seats about it, and commended the place for its retiredness.

And having understood by John Penderel that the Lord Wilmot was at Mr. Whitgreave's house (for John knew not of his remove to Bentley) his majesty was desirous to let my lord hear of him, and that he intended to come to Moseley at night.

To this end John was sent on Sunday morning to Moseley, but finding my lord removed thence, was much troubled; and then acquainting Mr. Whitgreave and Mr. Huddleston that his majesty was returned to Boscobel, and the disaccommodation he had there, whereupon they both resolve to go with John to Bentley, where, having gained him an access to my lord, his lordship designed to attend the king that night at Moseley, and desired Mr. Whitgreave to meet his lordship at a place appointed about twelve of the clock, and Mr. Huddleston to nominate a place where he would attend his majesty about one of the clock the same night.

Upon this intelligence, my lord made stay of Mrs. Jane Lane's journey to Bristol, till his majesty's pleasure was known.

John Penderel returned to Boscobel in the afternoon, with intimation of this designed meeting with my lord at Moseley that night, and the place which was appointed by Mr. Huddleston where his majesty should be expected. But his majesty, having not recovered his late foot journey to Madeley, was not able without a horse to perform this to Moseley, which was about five miles distant from Boscobel, and near the midway from thence to Bentley.

It was therefore concluded that his majesty should ride upon Humphrey Penderel's mill-horse (for Humphrey was the miller of White Ladies mill). The horse was taken up from grass, and accoutred, not with rich trappings or furniture, befitting so great a king, but with a pitiful old saddle, and a worse bridle.

When his majesty was ready to take horse, Colonel Carlis humbly took leave of him, being so well known in the country, that his attendance upon his majesty would in all probability have proved rather a disservice than otherwise; however, his hearty prayers were not wanting for his majesty's preservation.

Thus then his majesty was mounted, and thus he rode towards Moseley, attended by all the honest brothers, William, John, Richard, Humphrey, and George Penderel, and Francis Yates; each of these took a bill or pike staff on his back, and some of them had pistols in their pockets; two marched before, and one on each side his majesty's horse, and two came behind aloof off; their design being this, that in case they should have been questioned or encountered but by five or six troopers, or such like small party, they would have showed their valour in defending, as well as they had done their fidelity in otherwise serving his majesty; and though it was midnight, yet they conducted his majesty through by-ways, for better security.

After some experience had of the horse, his majesty complained, 'it was the heaviest dull jade he ever rode on'; to which Humphrey (the owner of him) answered (beyond the usual capacity of a miller): 'My liege, can you blame the horse to go heavily, when he has the weight of three kingdoms on his back?'

When his majesty came to Penford mill, within two miles of Mr. Whitgreave's house, his guides desired him to alight and go on foot the rest of the way, for more security, the foot way being the more secure, and the nearer; and at last they arrived at the place appointed by Mr. Huddleston (which was a little grove of trees, in a close of Mr. Whitgreave's, called the Pit-Leasow), in order to his majesty's being privately conveyed into Mr. Whitgreave's house; William, Humphrey, and George, returned with the horse, the other three attended his majesty to the house; but his majesty, being gone a little way, had forgot (it seems) to bid farewell to William and the rest who were going back, so he called to them and said, ' My troubles make me forget myself; I thank you all !' and gave them his hand to kiss.

The Lord Wilmot, in pursuance of his own appointment, came to the meeting place precisely at his hour, where Mr. Whitgreave received him, and conveyed him to his old chamber; but hearing nothing of the king at his prefixed time gave occasion to suspect some misfortune might have befallen him, though the night was very dark and rainy, which might possibly be the occasion of so long stay; Mr. Whitgreave therefore leaves my lord in his chamber, and goes to Pit-Leasow, where Mr. Huddleston attended his majesty's coming; and about two hours after the time appointed his majesty came, whom Mr. Whitgreave and Mr. Huddleston conveyed, with much satisfaction, into the house to my lord, who expected him with great solicitude, and presently kneeled down and embraced his majesty's knees, who kissed my lord on the cheek, and asked him earnestly, 'What is become of Buckingham, Cleveland, and others?' To which my lord could give little satisfaction, but hoped they were in safety.

My lord soon after (addressing himself to Whitgreave and Mr. Huddleston) said: 'Though I have concealed my friend's name all this while, now I must tell you, this is my master, your master, and the master of us all,' not knowing that they understood it was the king; whereupon his majesty was pleased to give his hand to Mr. Whitgreave and Mr. Huddleston to kiss, and told them he had received such an account from my Lord Wilmot of their fidelity, that he should never forget it: and presently asked Mr. Whitgreave, 'Where is your secret place?' which being showed his majesty, he was well pleased therewith, and returning into my lord's chamber, sat down on the bedside, where his nose fell a-bleeding, and then pulled out of his pocket a handkerchief, suitable to the rest of his apparel, both coarse and dirty.

His majesty's attire, as was before observed in part, was then a leathern doublet, with pewter buttons, a pair of old green breeches, and a jump coat (as the country calls it) of the same green, a pair of his own stockings, with the tops cut off, because embroidered, and a pair of stirrup stockings, which were lent him at Madeley, and a pair of old shoes, cut and slashed to give ease to his feet, an old gray greasy hat, without a lining, a noggen shirt of the coarsest linen; his face and his hands made of a reechy complexion, by the help of the walnut-tree leaves.

Mr. Huddleston, observing the coarseness of his majesty's shirt to disease him much and hinder his rest, asked my lord if the king would be pleased to change his shirt, which his majesty condescended unto, and presently put off his coarse shirt and put on a flaxen one of Mr. Huddleston's, who pulled off his majesty's shoes and stockings, and put him on fresh stockings, and dried his feet, where he found somebody had innocently, but indiscreetly, applied white paper, which, with going on foot from the place where his majesty alighted to the house, was rolled betwixt his stockings and his skin, and served to increase rather than assuage the soreness of his feet.

Mr. Whitgreave had by this time brought up some biscuit and a bottle of sack; his majesty eat of the one, and drank a good glass of the other; and, being thus refreshed, was pleased to say cheerfully, 'I am now ready for another march; and if it shall please God once more to place me at the head of but eight or ten thousand good men, of one mind, and resolved to fight, I shall not doubt to drive these rogues out of my kingdoms.'

It was now break of the day on Monday morning the 8th of September, and his majesty was desirous to take some rest; to which purpose a pallet was carried into one of the secret places, where his majesty lay down, but rested not so well as his host desired, for the place was close and inconvenient, and durst not adventure to put him into any bed in an open chamber, for fear of a surprise by the rebels.

After some rest taken in the whole, his majesty got up, and was pleased to take notice of and salute Mr. Whitgreave's mother, and (having his place of retreat still ready) sat between whiles in a closet over the porch, where he might see those that passed the road by the house.

Before the Lord Wilmot betook himself to his dormitory, he conferred with Mr. Whitgreave, and advised that himself or Mr. Huddleston would be always vigilant about the house, and give notice if any soldiers came; 'and,' says this noble lord, 'if it should so fall out that the rebels have intelligence of your harbouring any of the king's party, and should therefore put you to any torture for confession, be sure you discover me first, which may haply in such case satisfy them, and preserve the king.' This was the expression and care of a loyal subject, worthy eternal memory.

On Monday, his majesty and my lord resolved to

dispatch John Penderel to Colonel Lane at Bentley, with directions for the colonel to send my lord's horses for him that night about midnight, and to expect him at the usual place. My lord accordingly goes to Bentley again, to make way for his majesty's reception there, pursuant to a resolution taken up by his majesty to go westward, under the protection of Mrs. Jane Lane's pass; it being most probable that the rebels wholly pursued his majesty northwards, and would not at all suspect him gone into the west.

This Monday afternoon, Mr. Whitgreave had notice that some soldiers were in the neighbourhood, intending to apprehend him, upon information that he had been at Worcester fight. The king was then laid down upon Mr. Huddleston's bed, but Mr. Whitgreave presently secures his royal guest in the secret place, and my lord also leaves open all the chamber doors, and goes boldly down to the soldiers, assuring them (as his neighbours also testified) that he had not been from home in a fortnight then last past; with which asseveration the soldiers were satisfied, and came not up stairs at all.

In this interval the rebels had taken a cornet in Cheshire, who came in his majesty's troop to White Ladies, and either by menaces, or some other way, had extorted this confession from him concerning the king (whom these bloodhounds sought with all possible diligence), that he came in company with his majesty to White Ladies, where the rebels had no small hopes to find him; whereupon they posted thither without ever drawing bit, almost killed their horses, and brought their faint-hearted prisoners with them.

Being come to White Ladies on Tuesday, they called for Mr. George Giffard, who lived in an apartment of the house, presented a pistol to his breast, and bade him confess where the king was, or he should presently die. Mr. Giffard was too loyal and too much a gentleman to be frightened into any infidelity, resolutely denies the knowing any more but that divers cavaliers came thither on Wednesday night, ate up their provision, and departed; and that he was as ignorant who they were, as whence they came, or whither they went; and begged, if he must die, that they would first give him leave to say a few prayers. One of these

E

villains answered, 'If you can tell us no news of
the king you shall say no prayers.' But his discreet answer did somewhat assuage the fury of their
leader. They used the like threats and violence
(mingled, notwithstanding, with high promises of
reward) to Mrs. Anne Andrew (to whose custody
some of the king's clothes, when he first took upon
him the disguise, were committed), who (like a true
virago) faithfully sustained the one, and loyally refused the other, which put the rebels into such a
fury, that they searched every corner of the house,
broke down much of the wainscot, and at last beat
the intelligencer severely for making them lose
their labours.

During this Tuesday, in my Lord Wilmot's ab-
sence, his majesty was for the most part attended
by Mr. Huddleston, Mr. Whitgreave being much
abroad in the neighbourhood, and Mrs. Whitgreave
below stairs, both inquisitive after news, and the
motions of the soldiery, in order to the preservation
of their royal guest. The old gentlewoman was
this day told by a countryman, who came to her
house, that he heard the king, upon his retreat,
had beaten his enemies at Warrington Bridge, and

that there were three kings come in to his assistance; which story she related to his majesty for divertisement, who smiling, answered, 'Surely they are the three Kings of Cologne come down from heaven, for I can imagine none else.'

The same day his majesty out of the closet window espied two soldiers, who passed by the gate in the road, and told Mr. Huddleston he knew one of them to be a Highlander, and of his own regiment; who little thought his king and colonel to be so near.

And his majesty, for entertainment of the time, was pleased to discourse with Mr. Huddleston the particulars of the battle of Worcester (the same in substance with what is before related); and by some words which his majesty let fall, it might easily be collected that his counsels had been too often sooner discovered to the rebels than executed by his loyal subjects.

Mr. Huddleston had under his charge young Sir John Preston, Mr. Thomas Playn, and Mr. Francis Reynolds, and on this Tuesday in the morning (the better to conceal his majesty's being in the house, and excuse his own more than usual long stay above stairs) pretended himself to be indisposed and afraid of the soldiers, and therefore set his scholars at several garret windows, and surveyed the roads, to watch and give notice when they saw any troopers coming. This service the youths performed very diligently all day; and at night when they were at supper, Sir John called upon his companions, and said (more truly than he imagined), 'Come, lads, let us eat lustily, for we have been upon the life-guard to-day.'

This very day (September the 9th), the rebels at Westminster (in further pursuance of their bloody designs) set forth a proclamation for the discovery and apprehending Charles Stuart (for so their frontless impudence usually styled his sacred majesty), his adherents and abettors, with promise of £1000 reward to whomsoever should apprehend him (so vile a price they set upon so inestimable a jewel); and, besides, gave strict command to all officers of port towns, that they should permit no person to pass beyond sea without special license. 'And Saul sought David every day; but God delivered him not into his hand.'

On Tuesday night, between twelve and one

o'clock, the Lord Wilmot sent Colonel Lane to attend his majesty to Bentley; Mr. Whitgreave meets the colonel at the place appointed, and brings him to the corner of his orchard, where the colonel thought fit to stay whilst Mr. Whitgreave goes in and acquaints the king that he was come; whereupon his majesty took his leave of Mrs. Whitgreave, saluted her, and gave her many thanks for his entertainment, but was pleased to be more particular with Mr. Whitgreave and Mr. Huddleston, not only by giving them thanks, but by telling them he was very sensible of the dangers they might incur by entertaining him, if it should chance to be discovered to the rebels; therefore his majesty advised them to be very careful of themselves, and gave them direction to repair to a merchant in London, who should have order to furnish them with moneys and means of conveyance beyond sea, if they thought fit.

After his majesty had vouchsafed these gracious expressions to Mr. Whitgreave and Mr. Huddleston, they told his majesty all the service they could now do him was to pray heartily to Almighty God for his safety and preservation; and then kneeling down his majesty gave them his hand to kiss, and so went down stairs with them into the orchard, where Mr. Whitgreave both humbly and faithfully delivered his great charge into Colonel Lane's hands, telling the colonel who the person was he there presented to him.

The night was both dark and cold, and his majesty's clothing thin; therefore Mr. Huddleston humbly offered his majesty a cloak, which he was pleased to accept, and wore to Bentley, from whence Mr. Huddleston afterwards received it.

As soon as Mr. Whitgreave and Mr. Huddleston heard his majesty was not only got safe to Bentley, but marched securely from thence, they began to reflect upon his advice, and lest any discovery should be made of what had been acted at Moseley, they both absented themselves from home; the one went to London, the other to a friend's house in Warwick-shire, where they lived privately till such time as they heard his majesty was safely arrived in France, and that no part of the aforesaid transactions at Moseley had been discovered to the rebels, and then returned home.

This Mr. Whitgreave was descended of the ancient

family of the Whitgreaves of Burton, in the county of Stafford, and was first a cornet, afterwards lieutenant to Captain Thomas Giffard, in the first war for his majesty King Charles the First.

Mr. John Huddleston was a younger brother of the renowned family of the house of Hutton-John, in the county of Cumberland, and was a gentleman volunteer in his late majesty's service, first under Sir John Preston the elder, till Sir John was rendered unserviceable by the desperate wounds he received in that service, and after under Colonel Ralph Pudsey at Newark.

His majesty being safely conveyed to Bentley by Colonel Lane, staid there but a short time, took the opportunity of Mrs. Jane's pass, and rode before her to Bristol, the Lord Wilmot attending, by another way, at a distance. In all which journey Mrs. Lane performed the part of a most faithful and prudent servant to his majesty, showing her observance when an opportunity would allow it, and at other times acting her part in the disguise with much discretion.

But the particulars of his majesty's arrival at Bristol, and the houses of several loyal subjects, both in Somersetshire, Dorsetshire, Wiltshire, Hampshire, and so to Brighthemston, in Sussex, where he, on the 15th of October 1651, took shipping, and landed securely in France the next morning; and the several accidents, hardships, and encounters, in all that journey, must be the admired subject of the Second Part of this history.

The very next day after his majesty left Boscobel, being Monday the 8th of September, two parties of rebels came thither, the one being part of the county troop, who searched the house with some civility; the other (Captain Broadway's men) did it with more severity, eat up their little store of provision, plundered the house of what was portable, and one of them presented a pistol to William Penderel, and much frighted my dame Joan; yet both parties returned as ignorant as they came of that intelligence they so greedily sought after.

This danger being over, honest William began to think of making satisfaction for the fat mutton, and accordingly tendered Mr. Staunton its worth in money; but Staunton understanding the sheep was killed for the relief of some honest cavaliers, who had been sheltered at Boscobel, refused to take the money, but wished much good it might do them.

These Penderels were of honest parentage, but mean degree; six brothers, born at Hobbal Grange, in the parish of Tong, and county of Salop; William, John, Richard, Humphrey, Thomas, and George. John, Thomas, and George were soldiers in the first war for King Charles I. Thomas was slain at Stow fight; William, as you have heard, was a servant at Boscobel; Humphrey, a miller, and Richard rented part of Hobbal Grange.

His majesty had not been long gone from Boscobel, but Colonel Carlis sent William Penderel to Mr. Humphrey Ironmonger, his old friend at Wolverhampton, who not only procured him a pass from some of the rebel commanders, in a disguised name, to go to London, but furnished him with money for his journey, by means whereof he got safe thither, and from thence into Holland, where he brought the first happy news of his majesty's safety to his royal sister the Princess of Orange.

This Colonel William Carlis was born at Bromhall, in Staffordshire, within two miles of Boscobel, of good parentage, was a person of approved valour, and en-

gaged all along in the first war for King Charles I. of
happy memory, and since his death was no less active
for his royal son; for which, and his particular service and fidelity before mentioned, his majesty was
pleased, by letters patents under the great seal of
England, to give him, by the name of William Carlos
(which in Spanish signifies Charles), this very honour-
able coat of arms, *in perpetuam rei memoriam*, as 'tis
expressed in the letters patents. 'He bears upon
an oak proper in a field Or a Fess Gules, charged
with three Regal Crowns of the Second; by the
name of Carlos. And for his Crest a Civic Crown,
or oaken garland, with a sword and scepter crossed
through it saltier-wise.'

The oak is now properly called 'The Royal Oak
of Boscobel,' nor will it lose that name whilst it con-
tinues a tree, nor that tree a memory whilst we have
an inn left in England; since the 'Royal Oak' is
now become a frequent sign, both in London and all
the chief cities of this kingdom. And since his
majesty's happy restauration, that these mysteries
have been revealed, hundreds of people for many
miles round have flocked to see the famous Boscobel,
which (as you have heard) had once the honour to

be the palace of his sacred majesty, but chiefly to
behold the Royal Oak, which had been deprived of
all its young boughs by the numerous visitors of it,
who keep them in memory of his majesty's happy
preservation, insomuch that Mr. Fitzherbert, who was
afterwards proprietor, was forced in a due season of
the year to crop part of it, for its preservation, and
put himself to the charge of fencing it about with a
high pale, the better to transmit the happy memory
of it to posterity.

This Boscobel House has yet been a third time
fortunate; for after Sir George Booth's forces were
routed in Cheshire, in August 1659, the Lord Brere-
ton, who was engaged with him, took sanctuary there
for some time, and was preserved.

When his majesty was thus happily conveyed
away by Colonel Lane and his sister, the rebels had
an intimation that some of the brothers were instru-
mental in his preservation, so that, besides the
temptations Humphrey overcame at Shefnal, William
Penderel was twice questioned at Shrewsbury on
the same account by Captain Fox, and one Lluellin,
a sequestrator, and Richard was much threatened by
a peevish neighbour at White Ladies; but neither

threats nor temptations were able to batter the fort
of their loyalty.

After this unhappy defeat of his majesty's army
at Worcester, good God! in what strange canting
language did the fanaticks communicate their exulta-
tions to one another, particularly in a letter (hypo-
critically pretended to be written from the Church
of Christ at Wrexham, and printed in the Diurnal,
November 10, 1651) there is this malignant expression : 'Christ has revealed his own arm, and broke
the arm of the mighty once and again,' and now
lastly at Worcester; so that we conclude (in Ezekiel's
phrase) 'there will be found no roller to bind the late
king's arm to hold a sword again,' etc. And that
you may know who these false prophets were, the
letter was thus subscribed : 'Daniel Lloyd, Mor.
Lloyd, John Brown, Edw. Taylor, An. Maddokes,
Dav. Maurice'; men who measured causes by that
success which fell out according to their evil
desires, not considering that God intended, in
his own good time, 'to establish the king's throne
with justice.'

After the 'king had entered into the kingdom,
and returned to his own land,' the five brothers

attended him at Whitehall, on Wednesday the 13th
of June 1660, when his majesty was pleased to own
their faithful service, and graciously dismissed them
with a princely reward.

And soon after Mr. Huddleston and Mr. Whitgreave made their humble addresses to his majesty,
from whom they likewise received a gracious acknow-
ledgment of their service and fidelity to him at Moseley, and this in so high a degree of gratitude, and
with such a condescending frame of spirit, not at all
puffed up with prosperity, as cannot be paralleled in
the best of kings.

Here let us with all glad and thankful hearts
humbly contemplate the admirable providence of
Almighty God, who contrived such wonderful ways,
and made use of such mean instruments, for the preservation of so great a person. Let us delight to
reflect minutely on every particular, and especially
on such as most approach to miracle ; let us sum up
the number of those who were privy to this first and
principal part of his majesty's disguise and concealment: Mr. Giffard, the five Penderels, their mother,
and three of their wives, Colonel Carlos, Francis
Yates, and his wife, divers of the inhabitants

of White Ladies (which then held five several families), Mr. Woolf, his wife, son, daughter, and maid, Mr. Whitgreave and his mother, Mr. Huddleston, Colonel Lane and his sister; and then consider whether it were not indeed a miracle, that so many men and (which is far more) so many women should faithfully conceal so important and unusual a secret; and this notwithstanding the temptations and promises of reward on the one hand, and the danger and menaces of punishment on the other.

To which I shall add but this one circumstance, that it was performed by persons for the most part of that religion which has long suffered under an imputation (laid on them by some mistaken zealots) of disloyalty to their sovereign.

And now, as we have thus thankfully commemorated the wonderful *preservation* of his majesty, what remains but that we should return due thanks and praises for his no less miraculous RESTORATION; who, after a long series of misfortunes, and variety of afflictions, after he had been hunted to and fro like a 'partridge upon the mountains,' was, in God's due time, appointed to sit, as his vicegerent, upon the throne of his ancestors, and called forth to govern his own people when they least expected him; for which all the nation, even all the three nations, had just cause to sing

Te Deum laudamus.

BOSCOBEL

OR THE HISTORY OF THE
MOST MIRACULOUS PRESERVATION OF

KING CHARLES THE SECOND

AFTER THE BATTLE OF WORCESTER
SEPTEMBER 3RD, 1651

PART II

PREFACE

THE First Part of this miraculous History I long since published, having the means to be well informed in all circumstances relating to it; the scene (whereon those great actions were performed) being my native country, and many of the actors my particular friends.

I did not then intend to have proceeded farther, presuming some of those worthy persons of the west (who were the happy instruments in this Second Part) would have given us that so much desired supplement; the rather, since the publication of the wonderful series of this great work, wherein the hand of God so miraculously appeared in preservation of 'him whom the Lord hath chosen,' must needs open the eyes and convert the hearts of the most disloyal.

But finding, in all this time, nothing done, and the world more greedy of it than ever young ladies were to read the conclusion of an amorous strange romance, after they had left the darling lover plunged into some dire misfortune, I have thus endeavoured to compleat the History.

Chiefly encouraged hereunto by an express from Lisbon, wherein 'tis certified that (besides the translation of the first part of *Boscobel* into French) Mr. Peter Giffard of White Ladies has lately made it speak Portugese, and presented it to the infanta, our most excellent queen, who was pleased to accept it with grace, and peruse it with passion, intimating her royal desire to see the particulars how the hand of Providence had led the great monarch of her heart out of the treacherous snares of so many rebels.

In this I dare not undertake to deliver so many particulars as in the former; for though the time of his majesty's stay in those western parts was longer, yet the places were more remote, and my Lord Wilmot (the principal agent) dead. But I will again confidently promise to write nothing but truth, as near as a severe scrutiny can inform me.

And, perhaps, a less exactness in circumstantials will better please some who (as I have heard) object against my former endeavours on this royal subject as too minutely written, and particulars set down of too mean a concern, for which I have yet the example of that renowned historian, Famian Strada,[1] to protect me, who writing of the Emperor Charles the Fifth, mentions what meat he fed on such a day, what clothes he wore another time, and gives this reason, 'that it pleases to know every thing that princes do,' especially when by a chain of providences, whose every link seems small and weak in its single self, so great a 'blessing' will at last be drawn in amongst us.

That part of this unparalleled relation of a king which here I undertake to deliver, may fitly, I think, be called, 'The Second Stage of the Royal Progress,' wherein as I am sure every good subject will be astonished to read the hardships and difficulties his majesty encountered in this long and perilous journey, so will they be even overjoyed to find him at last (by the conduct of Heaven) brought safe to Paris, where my humble endeavours leave him thus comforted by the prophet : 'Fear not, for the hand of Saul shall not find thee, and thou shalt be king over Israel.'

T. B.

[1] De Bello Belgico.

BOSCOBEL

OR THE

HISTORY OF KING CHARLES THE SECOND'S MOST MIRACULOUS PRESERVATION AFTER THE BATTLE OF WORCESTER

THE SECOND STAGE OF THE ROYAI PROGRESS

PART II

HE that well considers the admirable events particularised in the First Part of this History of his majesty's miraculous preservation, will be apt to think his evil genius had almost racked its invention to find out hardships and perils beyond human imagination, and that his good angel had been even tired out with contriving suitable means for his deliverance; yet, if you please (after you have sufficiently wondered and blessed God for the preservation you read there), proceed and admire the strange stupendous passages you shall find here; which when you have done with just and due attention, I cannot doubt but your thoughts will easily raise themselves into some holy extasy, and growing warm with often repeating their own reflections, break forth at last, and join your exclamations with all the true and hearty adorers of the divine Providence, 'Thou art great, O Lord, and dost wonderful things; thou art God alone!'

I shall not need, I hope, to bespeak my readers' patience for any long introduction, since all the compliment I intend, is humbly to kiss the pen and paper, which have the honour to be servants of this royal subject, and without farther ceremony begin.

Colonel John Lane having (as it has been related) safely conveyed his majesty from Moseley to his own house at Bentley, in Staffordshire, on Tuesday night, the 9th of September 1651, the Lord Wilmot was there ready to receive him, and after his majesty had eaten and conferred with my lord and the colonel of his intended journey towards Bristol the very next morning, he went to bed, though his rest was not like to be long; for at the very break of the day on Wednesday morning the colonel called up his majesty, and brought him a new suit and cloak, which he had provided for him, of country grey cloth, as near as could be contrived like the holyday suit of a farmer's son, which was thought fittest to carry on the disguise. Here his majesty quitted his leather doublet and green breeches for this new grey suit, and forsook his former name Will. Jones for that of Will. Jackson.

Thus, then, was the royal journey designed: the king, as a tenant's son (a quality far more convenient for their intention than that of a direct servant), was ordered to ride before Mrs. Jane Lane as her attendant, Mr. Henry Lassels (who was kinsman, and had been coronet to the colonel in the late wars) to ride single, and Mr. John Petre of Horton in Buckinghamshire, and his wife, the colonel's sister, who were then accidentally at Bentley, being bound homeward, to ride in the same company; Mr. Petre and his wife little suspecting Will. Jackson, their fellow-traveller, to be the monarch of Great Britain.

His majesty thus refreshed and thus accoutred with all necessaries for a journey in the designed equipage, after he had taken leave of my Lord Wilmot, and agreed on their meeting within a few days after at Mr. George Norton's house at Leigh, near Bristol; the colonel conveyed him a back way into the stable, where he fitted his stirrups, and gave him some instructions for better acting the part of Will. Jackson, mounted him on a good double gelding, and directed him to come to the gate of the house, which he punctually performed, with his hat under his arm.

By this time it was twilight, and old Mrs. Lane (who knew nothing of this great secret) would needs see her beloved daughter take horse, which whilst she was intending, the colonel said to the king, 'Will, thou must give my sister thy hand'; but his majesty (unacquainted with such little offices) offered his hand the contrary way, which the old gentlewoman taking notice of, laughed, and asked the colonel her son, 'What a goodly horseman her daughter had got to ride before her?'

Mr. Petre and his wife, and Mr. Lassels being also mounted, the whole company took their journey (under the protection of the King of kings) towards Stratford-upon-Avon, in Warwickshire. And soon after they were gone from Bentley, the Lord Wilmot, Colonel Lane, and Robert Swan my lord's servant, took horse, with a hawk and spaniels with them for a disguise, intending to go that night to Sir Clement Fisher's house at Packington, in Warwickshire, where the colonel knew they should both be as welcome as generosity, and as secure as fidelity could make them.

When the king and his small retinue arrived near Wotton, within four miles of Stratford, they espied a troop of rebels, baiting (as they conceived) almost a mile before them in the very road, which caused a council to be held among them, wherein Mr. Petre presided, and he would by no means go on, for fear of losing his horse, or some other detriment; so that they wheeled about a more indirect way; and at Stratford (where they were of necessity to pass the river Avon) met the same or another troop in a narrow passage, who very fairly opened to the right and left, and made way for the travellers to march through them.

That night (according to designment) Mrs. Lane and her company took up their quarters at Mr. Tombs' house, at Longmarston, some three miles west of Stratford, with whom she was well acquainted. Here Will. Jackson being in the kitchen,

in pursuance of his disguise, and the cook maid
busy in providing supper for her master's friends,
she desired him to wind up the jack; Will. Jackson
was obedient, and attempted it, but hit not the
right way, which made the maid in some passion
ask, 'What countryman are you, that you know not
how to wind up a jack?' Will. Jackson answered
very satisfactorily, 'I am a poor tenant's son of
Colonel Lane, in Staffordshire; we seldom have
roast-meat, but when we have, we don't make use
of a jack'; which in some measure assuaged the
maid's indignation.

The same night my lord, with the colonel, arrived
safely at Sir Clement Fisher's house at Packington,
where they found a welcome suitable to the noble-
ness of his mind, and a security answerable to the
faithfulness of his heart.

Next morning my lord thought fit to dispatch
the colonel to London, to procure, if possible, a
pass for the king, by the name of William Jackson,
to go into France, and to bring it himself, or send
it (as opportunity should be offered) to Mr. Norton's
house, where my lord (as you have heard) was
designed to attend his majesty.

On Thursday morning (11th of September), the king, with Mrs. Lane and Mr. Lassels, rose early, and after Mrs. Lane had taken leave both of Mr. Petre and his wife (whose way lay more south) and of Mr. Tombs, the master of the house, they took horse, and without any considerable accident rode by Camden, and arrived that night at an inn in Cirencester, in Gloucestershire, distant about twenty-four miles from Longmarston. After supper, a good bed was provided for Mr. Lassels, and a truckle bed for Will. Jackson in the same chamber; but Mr. Lassels, after the chamberlain had left them, laid his majesty in the best bed, and himself in the other, and used the like due observance when any opportunity would allow it.

The next day, being Friday, the royal traveller, with his attendants, left Cirencester, and by the way of Sudbury rode to and through the city of Bristol (wherein they had once lost their way, till inquiry better informed them), and arrived that evening at Mr. Norton's house, at Leigh, some three miles from Bristol, and about thirty from Cirencester, which was the desired end of this perilous journey.

At this place his majesty still continued under the notion of one of Colonel Lane's tenants' sons, and, by a presettled contrivance with Mrs. Lane, feigned himself sick of an ague, under colour whereof she procured him the better chamber and accommodation without any suspicion, and still took occasion from thence, with all possible care and observance, to send the sick person some of the best meat from Mr. Norton's table; and Mrs. Norton's maid, Margaret Rider, who was commanded to be his nurse-keeper, and believed him sick indeed, made William a carduus posset, and was very careful of him; nor was his majesty at all known or suspected here, either by Mr. Norton or his lady, from whose knowledge yet he was not concealed out of any the least distrust of their fidelity, for his whole dominions yielded not more faithful subjects, but because such knowledge might haply at unawares have drawn a greater respect and observance from them than that exigent would safely admit of.

Under the disguise of this ague, his majesty for the most part kept his chamber during his stay at Leigh; yet, being somewhat wearied with that kind of imprisonment, one day, when his ague might be imagined to be in the intermission, he walked down to a place where the young men played at a game of ball called fives, where his majesty was asked by one of the gamesters if he could play, and would take his part at that game; he pleaded unskilfulness, and modestly refused.

But behold an unexpected accident here fell out, which put his majesty and Mrs. Lane into some apprehension of the danger of a discovery. Mr. Norton's butler, whose name was John Pope, had served a courtier some years before the war, and his majesty's royal father in the war, under Colonel Bagot, at Litchfield, and by that means had the physiognomy of the king, then Prince of Wales, so much imprinted in his memory, that, though his majesty was in all points most accurately disguised, yet the butler knew him, and communicated his knowledge to Mrs. Lane, who at first absolutely denied him to be the king, but after, upon conference and advice had with his majesty, it was thought best to acknowledge it to the butler, and, by the bonds of allegiance, conjure him to secrecy, who thereupon kissed the king's hand, and proved perfectly honest.

On Saturday night, 13th of September, the Lord Wilmot arrived at a village near Leigh, where he lay, but came every day to visit Wm. Jackson and Mrs. Lane, as persons of his acquaintance; and so had the opportunity to attend and consult with his majesty unsuspected during their stay at Leigh.

Soon after, upon serious advice had with my lord, it was resolved by his majesty to go to Trent, the house of Colonel Francis Wyndham, of whose fidelity his majesty had ample assurance, which lies in Somersetshire, but bordering on the very skirts of Dorsetshire, near Sherburn, and therefore was judged to be conveniently seated in the way towards Lime and other port towns, where his majesty might probably take shipping for France.

In pursuance of this resolve, the Lord Wilmot, as his majesty's harbinger, rode to Trent on Monday, to make way for his more private reception there; and Tuesday morning (September 16) his Majesty's ague being then, as was pretended, in the recess, he repaired to the stable, and there gave order for making ready the horses; and then it was signified from Mrs. Lane (though before so agreed) that William Jackson should ride single and carry the portmanteau; accordingly they mounted, being attended part of the way by one of Mr. Norton's men as a guide, and that day rode through the body of Somersetshire, to Mr. Edward Kirton's house at Castle Cary, near Burton, where his majesty lay that night, and next morning arrived at Colonel Wyndham's said house, which was about twenty-six miles from Leigh.

His majesty was now at Trent, in as much safety as the master of the house his fidelity and prudence could make him; but the great work was how to procure a vessel for transportation of this great treasure. For this end his majesty, the Lord Wilmot, Colonel Wyndham, had several consults; and in pursuance of their determination, the colonel, with his trusty servant Henry Peters, posted to Lime, which is about twenty miles from Trent, where, after some difficulty, by the assistance of Captain William Elsden, a loyal subject (at whose house the colonel lodged), he hired a bark to transport his majesty for France, which bark was by agreement to attend at Charmouth (a little maritime village near Lime) at a time appointed, and returned with all speed to Trent with the good news.

The next day his majesty resolved for Lime, and
Mrs. Jane Lane here humbly took her leave of him,
returning with Mr. Lassels, by his majesty's permission, into Staffordshire, leaving him in faithful
hands, and in a hopeful way of escaping the bloody
designs of merciless rebels, which as it was all along
the scope of her endeavours, so was it now the
subject of her prayers; yet it was still thought the
best disguise for his majesty to ride before some
woman, and accordingly Mrs. Julian Coningsby,
Colonel Wyndham's kinswoman, had the honour to
ride behind his majesty, who with the Lord Wilmot,
the colonel, and Henry Peters, came that evening
to a blind inn in Charmouth, near which place the
skipper had promised to be in readiness with his
bark; but observe the disappointment.

In the interim (whilst Colonel Wyndham was
gone back to Trent) it seems the rebels' proclamation for apprehending Charles Stuart (meaning, in
their impudent phrase, our then gracious king), and
prohibiting, for a certain time, the transportation
of any person without a particular license, had been
published in and about Lime; and the skipper
having acquainted his wife that he had agreed to

transport two or three persons into France, whom he believed might be cavaliers, it seems the grey mare was the better horse, for she locked up her husband in his chamber, and would by no means permit him to go the voyage; so that whilst Henry Peters staid on the beach most part of the night, his majesty and the rest of the company sate up in the inn, expecting news of the seaman with his boat, who never appeared.

The next morning, his majesty and attendants resolving to return to Trent, rode first to Bruteport, in Dorsetshire, where he stayed at an inn, whilst Henry Peters was sent back to Captain Elsden, to see if there were any hope left of persuading the skipper, or rather of gaining leave of his wife, for him to undertake the voyage; but all endeavours proved ineffectual, and by that time Harry returned, the day was so far spent that his majesty could conveniently reach no farther that night than Broad-Windsor; and (which added much to the danger) Colonel Heane (one of Cromwell's commanders) at this very time was marching rebels from several garrisons to Weymouth and other adjacent ports, in order to their being shipped, for the forcing the island of Jersey from his majesty's obedience, as they had done all the rest of his dominions; so that the roads of this country were full of soldiers.

Broad-Windsor afforded but one inn, and that the George, a mean one too, and (which was worse) the best accommodations in it were, before his majesty's arrival, taken up by rebel soldiers, one of whose doxies was brought to bed in the house, which caused the constable and overseers for the poor of the parish to come thither at an unseasonable hour of the night, to take care that the brat might not be left to the charge of the parish; so that his majesty, through this disturbance, went not to bed at all; and we may safely conclude he took as little rest here as he did the night before at Charmouth. Thus were 'the tribulations of David's heart enlarged,' and he prayed, 'Deliver me, O Lord, from my distresses.'

His majesty having still thus miraculously escaped dangers which hourly environed him, returned safe to Trent next morning, where, after some refreshment and rest taken, he was pleased to call my Lord Wilmot and Colonel Wyndham (the members of his little privy council) together, to consider what way was next to be attempted for his transportation.

After several proposals, it was at last resolved that my lord (attended and conducted by Henry Peters) should the next day be sent to Salisbury to Mr. John Coventry (son to the late Lord Coventry, lord keeper of the great seal of England), who then lived in the close of that city, and was known to be both a prudent person and a perfect lover of his sovereign, as well to advise how to procure a bark for passing his majesty into France, as for providing some moneys for his present necessary occasions.

My lord, being arrived at Salisbury, dispatched Henry Peters back to Trent, with intimation of the good reception he found there; for Mr. Coventry did not only furnish him with moneys, but was very solicitous for his majesty's safety; to which end he advised with Dr. Humphrey Henchman, a worthy divine, who, since his majesty's happy restauration, was with much merit advanced to the episcopal see of Salisbury.

The result of these two loyal persons' consultation was, that his majesty should be desired to remove to Hele (which lay about three miles north-

east of Salisbury), the dwelling-house of Mrs. Mary
Hyde, the relict of Laurence Hyde, Esq., eldest
brother to Hon. Sir Robert Hyde, one of the
justices of his majesty's Court of Common Pleas,
whom they knew to be both as discreet and as
loyal as any of her sex.

With this resolution and advice, Mr. Coventry
dispatched his chaplain, Mr. John Selleck, to Trent,
with a letter, rolled up into the bigness of a musket
bullet, which the faithful messenger had order to
swallow down his throat in case of any danger.

Meantime Mr. Coventry had found out a trusty
seaman at Southampton, who undertook to transport whom he pleased; but on second thoughts
and advice had with my Lord Wilmot, it was not
held safe for his majesty to take shipping there, in
regard of the so many castles by which the ships
pass that are outward-bound, and the often examina-
tion of the passengers in them; so that some of
the small ports of Sussex were concluded to be the
safer places for effecting this great work of his
majesty's delivery from the hands of such unparalleled rebels, who even ravenously thirsted
after royal blood.

In the interim Mr. Selleck returned with his majesty's resolution to come to Hele, signified by a like paper bullet; and by this time his majesty thought fit to admit of the service and assistance of Colonel Robert Philips (grandson to the famed Sir Edward Philips, late master of the rolls), who lived in those parts, and was well acquainted with the ways of the country, and known to be as faithful as loyalty could make him. This colonel undertook to be his majesty's conductor to Hele, which was near thirty miles distant from Trent.

During his majesty's stay at Trent (which was about a fortnight), he was, for his own security, forced to confine himself to the voluntary imprisonment of his chamber, which was happily accommodated (in case the rebels had searched the house) with an old well-contrived secret place, long before made (for a shelter against the inquisition of pursuivants) by some of the ancient family of the Gerhards, Colonel Wyndham's lady's ancestors, who were recusants, and had formerly been owners of that house.

His majesty's meat was likewise (to prevent the danger of a discovery) for the most part dressed

in his own chamber, the cookery whereof served
him for some divertisement of the time; and it is
a great truth if we say, there was no cost spared,
nor care wanting in the colonel, for the entertainment and preservation of his royal guest.

On the 3rd of October, his majesty (having given
Colonel Wyndham particular thanks for his great
care and fidelity towards him) left Trent, and began
his journey with Colonel Philips, and personating a
tenant's son of his, towards Hele, attended by
Henry Peters (afterwards yeoman of the field to
his majesty), and riding before Mrs. Coningsby.
The travellers passed by Wincanton, and near the
midst of that day's journey arrived at Mere, a little
market town in Wiltshire, and dined at the George
inn; the hoast, Mr. Christopher Philips, whom the
colonel knew to be perfectly honest.

The hoast sate at the table with his majesty, and
administered matters of discourse, told the colonel,
for news, that he heard the men of Westminster
(meaning the rebels), notwithstanding their victory
at Worcester, were in a great maze, not knowing
what was become of the king; but (says he) it is
the most received opinion that he is come in a

disguise to London, and many houses have been searched for him there: at which his majesty was observed to smile.

After dinner, mine hoast familiarly asked the king 'if he were a friend to Cæsar?' to which his majesty answered, 'Yes.' 'Then,' said he, 'here's a health to King Charles,' in a glass of wine, which his majesty and the colonel both pledged; and that evening arrived in safety at Hele. And his majesty, since his happy return, has been pleased to ask, 'What has become of his honest hoast at Mere?'

In the mean time the Lord Wilmot (who took up the borrowed name of Mr. Barlow) rode to such gentlemen of his acquaintance in Hampshire, whom he knew to be faithful subjects, to seek means for (what he so much desired) the transportation of his majesty; and first repaired to Mr. Lawrence Hyde (a name as faithful as fortunate in his majesty's service), at his house at Hinton d'Aubigny, near Catharington, then to Mr. Thomas Henslow, at Burhant, in the same county, to whom (as persons of known fidelity) my lord communicated his weighty business, and desired their assistance for procuring a bark for his majesty's transportation.

Mr. Henslow (in zeal to this service) immediately acquainted the Earl of Southampton (then at his house at Titchfield, and afterwards with much merit dignified with the great office of lord high treasurer of England) with this most important affair, my Lord Wilmot judging it fitter for Mr. Henslow (his neighbour) to do it, than for himself, in those circumstances, to appear at my lord's house, whose eminent fidelity and singular prudence, in the conduct of even the greatest affairs of state, being known both to them and all the world, and his great power and command at Bewly Haven, and the maritime parts of Hampshire, esteemed very favourable for their design, wherein his lordship was extremely active and solicitous.

Besides this, Mr. Lawrence Hyde recommended my Lord Wilmot to Colonel George Gunter, who lived at Rackton, near Chichester, in Sussex, and was known to be both faithful and active, not unlike to be successful in this service, to whom therefore my lord hasted, and lay at Rackton one night, where he imparted his great solicitation to the colonel and his kinsman, Mr. Thos. Gunter, who was then accidentally there.

All these persons had the like instructions from my lord, which made a deep impression on their loyal hearts, and excited them to use their utmost endeavours by several ways and means to procure the Noah's ark, which might at last secure his majesty from the great inundation of rebellion and treason which then did overspread the face of his whole dominions.

But to return to my humble observance of his majesty at Hele, where Mrs. Hyde was so transported with joy and loyalty towards him, that at supper, though his majesty was set at the lower end of the table, yet the good gentlewoman had much adoe to overcome herself, and not to carve to him first; however she could not refrain from drinking to him in a glass of wine, and giving him two larks, when others had but one.

After supper, Mr. Frederick Hyde (brother-in-law to the widow, who was then at Hele, and since created serjeant-at-law) discoursed with his majesty upon various subjects, not suspecting who he was, but wondered to receive such rational discourse from a person whose habit spoke him but of mean degree; and when his majesty was brought to his chamber, Dr. Henchman attended him there, and had a long and private communication with him.

Next day it was thought fit, to prevent the danger of any discovery, or even suspicion in the house, that in regard his majesty might possibly stay there some days before the conveniency of a transportation could be found out, he should that day publickly take his leave, and ride about two miles from the house, and then be privately brought in again the same evening, when all the servants were at supper; which was accordingly performed, and after that time his majesty appeared no more at Hele in publick, but had meat brought him privately to his chamber, and was attended by the good widow with much care and observance.

Now among the many faithful solicitors for this long-expected bark, Colonel Gunter happened to be the lucky man who first procured it at Brighthemston, in Sussex, by the assistance of Mr. Francis Mansel, merchant of Chichester, and the concurrent endeavours of Mr. Thos. Gunter; and on Saturday night, the 11th of October, he brought the happy tidings to my Lord Wilmot and Colonel Philips, who then lay, the one at Mr. Lawrence Hyde's, the other at Mr. Anthony Brown's house, his neighbour and tenant.

The next morning, being Sunday, Colonel Philips was dispatched to Hele with the much-desired news, and with instructions to attend his majesty on Monday to the Downs, called Old Winchester, near Warnford.

Early in the morning his majesty was privately conveyed from Hele, and went on foot at least two miles to Clarendon Park Corner, attended by Dr. Henchman, then took horse with Colonel Philips; and at the appointed time and place, the Lord Wilmot, Colonel Gunter, and Mr. Thomas Gunter, met his majesty, with a brace of greyhounds, the better to carry on the disguise.

That night, though both Mr. Lawrence Hyde and Mr. Henslow had each of them provided a secure lodging for his majesty, by the Lord Wilmot's order, yet it was judged fittest by Colonel Gunter, and accordingly agreed unto by my lord, that his majesty should lodge at Mr. Thomas Symons's house at Hambledon, in Hampshire, who married the colonel's sister, in regard the colonel knew them to be very faithful, but chiefly because it lay

more directly in the way from Hele to Brighthemston; and accordingly Colonel Gunter attended his
majesty to his sister's house that night, who provided a good supper for them, though she had not
the least suspicion or intimation of his majesty's
presence among them.

The king and his small retinue arriving in safety
at Mrs. Symons's house on Monday night the 13th
of October, were heartily welcomed by Mrs. Symons,
for her husband was not then at home; but by
that time they had sup'd, in comes Mr. Symons, who
wondering to see so many strangers in his house, was
assured by his brother Gunter that they were all
honest gentlemen; yet, at first interview, he much
suspected Mr. Jackson to be a roundhead, observing
how little hair William Penderel's scissors had left
him; but at last being fully satisfied they were all
cavaliers, he soon laid open his heart, and thought
nothing too good for them, was sorry his beer was
no stronger, and, to encourage it, fetched down a
bottle of strong water, and, mixing it with the beer,
drank a cheerful cup to Mr. Jackson, calling him
'brother roundhead,' whom his majesty pledged;
who was here observed to be cloathed in a short

juppa of a sad-coloured cloth, and his breeches of another species, with a black hat, and without cuffs, somewhat like the meaner sort of country gentlemen.

Mr. Symons, in the time of entertaining his guests, did by chance let fall an oath, for which Mr. Jackson took occasion modestly to reprove him.

His majesty, thus resting himself Monday night at Hambledon, early on Tuesday morning (October the 14th) prepared for his journey to Brighthemston distant about thirty-five miles from thence. But (having then no further use for Colonel Philips) dismissed him with thanks for his fidelity and service, in this most secret and important affair; and then, having also bidden farewell to Mr. Symons and his wife, took horse, attended by my Lord Wilmot and his man, Colonel Gunter, and Mr. Thomas Gunter.

When they came near the Lord Lumley's house at Stanstead, in Sussex, it was considered that the greatness of the number of horse might possibly raise some suspicion of them: Mr. Thomas Gunter was therefore dismissed with thanks for the service he had done, and his majesty held on his journey

without any stay; and being come to Bramber,
within seven miles of the desired port, met there
some of Colonel Herbert Morley's soldiers, who yet
did neither examine, nor had they, as far as could
be discerned, the least suspicion of the royal passengers, who arrived at last at the George inn in
Brighthemston, where Mr. Francis Mansel, who
assisted Colonel Gunter in this happy service, had
agreed to meet him.

At supper Mr. Mansel sate at the upper end of the
table, and Mr. Jackson (for that name his majesty
still retained) at the lower end. The innkeeper's
name was Smith, and had formerly been related to
the court, so that he suspected Mr. Jackson to be
whom he really was; which his majesty understanding, he discoursed with his hoast after supper,
whereby his loyalty was confirmed, and the man
proved faithful.

The next morning, being Wednesday, October
the 15th (the same day on which the noble Earl
of Derby became a royal martyr at Boulton), his
majesty, having given particular thanks to Colonel
Gunter for his great care, pains, and fidelity towards
him, took shipping with the Lord Wilmot in the

bark which lay in readiness for him at that harbour, and whereof Mr. Nicholas Tetersal was owner; and the next day, with an auspicious gale of wind, landed safely at Fecam, near Havre de Grace, in Normandy; where his majesty might happily say with David, ' Thou hast delivered me from the violent man; therefore will I sing praises to thy name, O Lord.'

This very bark, after his majesty's happy restauration, was by Captain Tetersal brought into the river Thames, and lay some months at anchor before Whitehall, to renew the memory of the happy service it had performed.

His majesty, having nobly rewarded Captain Tetersal in gold for his transportation, lodged this night at an inn in Fecam, and the next day rode to Roan, still attended by the faithful Lord Wilmot, where he continued incognito several days at Mr. Scot's house, since created baronet, till he had sent an express to the queen, his royal mother, who had been long solicitous to hear of his safety, and the court of France, intimating his safe arrival there, and had quitted his disguised habit for one more befitting the dignity of so great a king.

H

Upon the first intelligence of this welcome news, his highness the Duke of York sent his coach forthwith to attend his majesty at Roan, and the Lord Gerard, with others his majesty's servants, made all possible haste, with glad hearts, to perform their duty to him; so that on the 29th of October his majesty set forward towards Paris, lay that night at Fleury, about seven leagues from Roan; the next morning his royal brother, the Duke of York, was ready to receive him at Magnie, and that evening his majesty was met at Monceaux, a village near Paris, by the Queen of England, accompanied with her brother, the Duke of Orleans, and attended by a great number of coaches, and many both English and French lords and gentlemen on horseback, and was thus gladly conducted the same night, though somewhat late, to the Louvre at Paris, to the inexpressible joy of his dear mother the Queen, his royal brother the Duke of York, and of all true hearts.

Here we must again, with greater reason, humbly contemplate the admirable providence of Almighty God, which certainly never appeared more miraculously than in this strange deliverance of his majesty from such an infinity of dangers, that history itself cannot produce a parallel, nor will posterity willingly believe it.

From the 3rd of September at Worcester, to the 15th of October at Brighthemston, being one and forty days, he passed through more dangers than he travelled miles, of which yet he traversed in that time only near three hundred (not to speak of his dangers at sea, both at his coming into Scotland, and his going out of England, nor of his long march from Scotland to Worcester), sometimes on foot with uneasy shoes; at other times on horseback, encumbered with a portmanteau; and which was worse, at another time on the gall-backed, slow-paced, miller's horse; sometime acting one disguise in coarse linen and a leather doublet, sometimes another of almost as bad a complection; one day he is forced to sculk in a barn at Madeley, another day sits with Colonel Carlos in a tree, with his feet extreamly galled, and at night glad to lodge with William Penderel in a secret place at Boscobel, which never was intended for the dormitory of a king.

Sometimes he was forced to shift with coarse fare for a bellyful; another time in a wood, glad to relieve

the necessities of nature with a mess of milk, served
up in an homely dish by good-wife Yates, a poor
country woman; then again, for a variety of tribula-
tion, when he thought himself almost out of danger,
he directly meets some of those rebels who so
greedily sought his blood, yet, by God's great providence, had not the power to discover him; and
(which is more than has yet been mentioned) he
sent at another time to some subjects for relief and
assistance in his great necessity, who out of a
pusillanimous fear of the bloody arch-rebel then
reigning durst not own him.

Besides all this 'twas not the least of his afflictions daily to hear the Earl of Derby, and other his
loyal subjects, some murdered, some imprisoned,
and others sequestered in heaps, by the same
bloody usurper, only for performing their duty to
their lawful king. In a word, there was no kind of
misery (but death itself) of which his majesty, in
this horrible persecution, did not in some measure,
both in body, mind, and estate bear a very great
share; yet such was his invincible patience in this
time of tryal, such his fortitude, that he overcame
them all with such pious advantage to himself, that

their memory is now sweet, and 'it was good for him that he had been afflicted.'

Of these his majesty's sufferings and forced extermination from his own dominions, England's great chancellor thus excellently descants:

'We may tell those desperate wretches, who yet harbour in their thoughts wicked designs against the sacred person of the king, in order to the compassing their own imaginations, that God Almighty would not have led him through so many wildernesses of afflictions of all kinds, conducted him through so many perils by sea, and perils by land, snatched him out of the midst of this kingdom when it was not worthy of him, and when the hands of his enemies were even upon him, when they thought themselves so sure of him, that they would bid so cheap and so vile a price for him. He would not in that article have so covered him with a cloud, that he travelled even with some pleasure and great observation through the midst of his enemies: He would not so wonderfully have new modelled that army; so inspired their hearts, and the hearts of the whole nation, with an honest and impatient longing for the return of their dear sovereign, and in the meantime have exercised him (which had little less of providence in it than the other) with those unnatural, or at least unusual, disrespects and reproaches abroad, that he might have a harmless and an innocent appetite to his own country, and return to his own people, with a full value, and the whole unwasted bulk of his affections, without being corrupted or byassed by extraordinary foreign obligations: God Almighty would not have done all this but for a servant whom he will always preserve as the apple of his own eye, and always defend from the most secret machinations of his enemies.'

Thus the best and happiest of orators.

Some may haply here expect I should have continued the particulars of this history to the time of his majesty's happy restauration, by giving an account of the reception his majesty found from the several princes beyond the seas, during his exile, and of his evenness of mind and prudent deportment towards them upon all occasions: but that was clearly beyond the scope of my intention, which aimed only to write the wonderful history of a great and good king, violently pursued in his own dominions by the worst of rebels, and miraculously preserved, under God, by the best of subjects.

In other countries, of which his majesty traversed not a few, he found kindness and a just compassion of his adversity from many, and from some a neglect and disregard; yet, in all the almost nine years abroad, I have not heard of any passage that approached the degree of a miracle like that at home; therefore I may, with faith to my own intentions, not improperly make a silent transition from his majesty's arrival at Paris, on the 13th day of October 1651, to his return to London on the 29th of May 1660; and, with a *Te Deum laudamus*, sum up all, and say with the prophet: 'My lord the king has come again in peace to his own house.' 'And all the people shouted, and said, God save the King!'

AN ACCOUNT

OF HIS MAJESTY'S ESCAPE FROM WORCESTER

DICTATED TO MR. PEPYS BY THE KING HIMSELF

AN ACCOUNT

OF HIS MAJESTY'S ESCAPE FROM WORCESTER

DICTATED TO MR. PEPYS BY THE KING

HIMSELF

To this narrative Mr. Pepys, has subjoined his own remarks and
many corrections and illustrations, procured from the King,
from Father Hodlestone, and from Colonel Philips. They
are inserted in the form of notes.

———

NEWMARKET, *Sunday, October 3rd, and
Tuesday, October 5th,* 1680.

AFTER that the battle was so absolutely lost as to
be beyond hope of recovery, I began to think of the
best way of saving myself; and the first thought
that came into my head was, that, if I could possibly, I would get to London, as soon, if not sooner,
than the news of our defeat could get thither: and
it being near dark, I talked with some, especially
with my Lord Rochester, who was then Wilmot,
about their opinions, which would be the best way
for me to escape, it being impossible, as I thought,
to get back into Scotland. I found them mightily

distracted, and their opinions different, of the possibility of getting to Scotland, but not one agreeing with mine, for going to London, saving my Lord Wilmot; and the truth is, I did not impart my design of going to London to any but my Lord Wilmot. But we had such a number of beaten men with us, of the horse, that I strove, as soon as ever it was dark, to get from them; and though I could not get them to stand by me against the enemy, I could not get rid of them, now I had a mind to it.

So we, that is, my Lord Duke of Buckingham, Lauderdale, Derby, Wilmot, Tom Blague, Duke Darcey, and several others of my servants, went along northward towards Scotland; and at last we got about sixty that were gentlemen and officers, and slipt away out of the high road that goes to Lancastershire, and kept on the right hand, letting all the beaten men go along the great road and ourselves not knowing very well which way to go, for it was then too late for us to get to London on horseback, riding directly for it; nor could we do it, because there was yet many people of quality with us that I could not get rid of.

So we rode through a town short of Woolverhampton, betwixt that and Worcester, and went through, there lying a troop of the enemies there that night. We rode very quietly through the town, they having nobody to watch, nor they suspecting us no more than we did them, which I learned afterwards from a country fellow. We went that night about twenty miles, to a place called White Ladys, hard by Tong Castle, by the advice of Mr. Giffard, where we stopt, and got some little refreshment of bread and cheese, such as we could get, it being just beginning to be day. This White Ladys was a private house that Mr. Giffard, who was a Staffordshire man, had told me belonged to honest people that lived thereabouts.[1]

[1] S. Pepys desiring to know from Father Hodlestone what he knew touching the brotherhood of the Penderells, as to the names and qualities of each of the brothers? He answered that he was not very perfect in it, but that as far as he could recollect they were thus—viz. :

1st, William, the eldest, who lived at Boscobel.

2nd, John, who lived at White Ladys, a kind of woodward there, all the brothers living in the wood, having little farms there, and labouring for their living, in cutting down of wood, and watching the wood from being stolen, having the benefit of some cowgrass to live on. Father Hodlestone farther told me, that here lived one Mr. Walker, an old gentleman, a priest, whither the poor

And just as we came thither, there came in a country fellow, that told us there were three thousand of our horse just hard by Tong Castle, upon the heath, all in disorder, under David Leslie, and some other of the general officers : upon which there were some of the people of quality that were with me who were very earnest that I should go to him, and endeavour to go into Scotland ; which I thought was absolutely impossible, knowing very well that the country would all rise upon us, and that men who had deserted me when they were in good order, would never stand to me when they have been beaten.

Catholics in that neighbourhood resorted for devotion, and whom Father Hodlestone used now and then to visit, and say prayers, and do holy offices with. Upon which score it was, that John Penderell happened to know him in the highway, when the said John Penderell was looking out for a hiding-place for my Lord Wilmot. This John was he, as Father Hodlestone says, that took the most pains of all the brothers.

3rd, Richard, commonly called among them Trusty Richard, who lived the same kind of life with the rest.

4th, Humphrey, a miller, who has a son at this day [1680] footman to the Queen, to be heard of at Somerset House.

5th, George, another brother, who was in some degree less or more, as he remembers, employed in this service. He thinks there was a sixth brother, bu of that is not certain.— HODLESTONE.

This made me take the resolution of putting myself into a disguise, and endeavouring to get a-foot to London, in a country fellow's habit, with a pair of ordinary gray-cloth breeches, a leathern doublet, and a green jerkin, which I took in the house of White Ladys. I also cut my hair very short, and flung my clothes into a privy-house, that nobody might see that any body had been stripping themselves.[1] I acquainting none with my resolution of

---

[1] There were six brothers of the Penderells, who all of them knew the secret ; and (as I have since learned from one of them) the man in whose house I changed my clothes came to one of them about two days after, and asking him where I was, told him that they might get £1000 if they would tell, because there was that sum laid upon my head. But this Penderell was so honest, that, though he at that time knew where I was, he bade him have a care what he did ; for, that I being gone out of all reach, if they should now discover I had ever been there, they would get nothing but hanging for their pains. I would not change my clothes at any of the Penderell's houses, because I meant to make further use of them, and they might be suspected ; but rather chose to do it in a house where they were not papists, I neither knowing then, nor to this day what the man was at whose house I did it. But the Penderells have since endeavoured to mitigate the business of their being tempted by their neighbour to discover me ; but one of them did certainly declare it to me at that time.—KING.

Concerning one Yates, that married a sister of one of the Penderells, Father Hodlestone says, he has heard that the old coarse shirt, which the king had on, did belong to him ; and

going to London but my Lord Wilmot, they all
desiring me not to acquaint them with what I intended to do, because they knew not what they
might be forced to confess; on which consideration
they, with one voice, begged of me not to tell them
what I intended to do.

So all the persons of quality, and officers who
were with me (except my Lord Wilmot, with whom
a place was agreed upon for our meeting at London,
if we escaped, and who endeavoured to go on horseback, in regard, as I think, of his being too big to
go on foot), were resolved to go and join with the
three thousand disordered horse, thinking to get
away with them to Scotland. But, as I did before
believe, they were not marched six miles, after they
got to them, but they were all routed by a single
troop of horse; which shows that my opinion was
not wrong in not sticking to men who had ran
away.

As soon as I was disguised I took with me a
country fellow, whose name was Richard Penderell,
consequently that the king did shift himself at his house; but
believes that the rest of the king's clothes were William Penderell's,
he being a tall man, and the breeches the king had on being very
long at the knees.—HODL.

whom Mr. Giffard had undertaken to answer for to be an honest man. He was a Roman Catholic, and I chose to trust them, because I knew they had hiding-holes for priests, that I thought I might make use of in case of need.

I was no sooner gone (being the next morning after the battle, and then broad day) out of the house with this country fellow, but being in a great wood, I set myself at the edge of the wood, near the highway that was there, the better to see who came after us, and whither they made any search after the runaways, and I immediately saw a troop of horse coming by, which I conceived to be the same troop that beat our three thousand horse; but it did not look like a troop of the army's, but of the militia, for the fellow before it did not look at all like a soldier.

In this wood I staid all day, without meat or drink; and by great good fortune it rained all the time, which hindered them, as I believe, from coming into the wood to search for men that might be fled thither. And one thing is remarkable enough, that those with whom I have since spoken, of them that joined with the horse upon the heath, did say that it rained little or nothing with them all the day, but only in the wood where I was, this contributing to my safety.

As I was in the wood I talked with the fellow about getting towards London; and asking him many questions about what gentlemen he knew, I did not find he knew any man of quality in the way towards London. And the truth is, my mind changed as I lay in the wood, and I resolved of another way of making my escape; which was, to get over the Severn into Wales, and so to get either to Swansey, or some other of the sea-towns that I knew had commerce with France, to the end I might get over that way, as being a way that I thought none would suspect my taking; besides that, I remembered several honest gentlemen that were of my acquaintance in Wales.

So that night, as soon as it was dark, Richard Penderell and I took our journey on foot towards the Severn, intending to pass over a ferry, half-way between Bridgenorth and Shrewsbury. But as we were going in the night, we came by a mill where I heard some people talking (memorandum, that I had got some bread and cheese the night before at one of the Penderell's houses, I not going in), and as we conceived it was about twelve or one o'clock at night; and the country fellow desired me not to answer if any body should ask me any questions, because I had not the accent of the country.

Just as we came to the mill, we could see the miller, as I believe, sitting at the mill door, he being in white clothes, it being a very dark night. He called out, 'Who goes there?' Upon which Richard Penderell answered, 'Neighbours going home,' or some such-like words. Whereupon the miller cried out, 'If you be neighbours, stand, or I will knock you down.' Upon which, we believing there was company in the house, the fellow bade me follow him close, and he ran to a gate that went up a dirty lane, up a hill, and opening the gate, the miller cried out, 'Rogues! rogues!' And thereupon some men came out of the mill after us, which I believe were soldiers: so we fell a-running, both of us up the lane, as long as we could run, it being very deep and very dirty, till at last I bade him leap over a hedge, and lie still to hear if any body followed us; which we did, and continued lying down upon the ground about half an hour, when, hearing nobody come, we continued our way on to the village upon the Severn, where the fellow told me there was an honest gentleman, one Mr. Woolfe, that lived in that town,[1] where I might be with great safety, for that he had hiding-holes for priests. But I would not go in till I knew a little of his mind, whether he would receive so dangerous a guest as me, and therefore stayed in a field, under a hedge, by a great tree, commanding him not to say it was I, but only to ask Mr. Woolfe whether he would receive an English gentleman, a person of quality, to hide him the next day, till we could travel again by night, for I durst not go but by night.

Mr. Woolfe, when the country fellow told him that it was one that had escaped from the battle of Worcester, said that, for his part, it was so dangerous a thing to harbour any body that was known, that he would not venture his neck for any man, unless it were the king himself. Upon which, Richard Penderell, very indiscreetly, and without any leave, told him that it was I. Upon which Mr. Woolfe replied, that he should be very ready to

---

1 Mr. Francis Woolfe lived at Madely.—HODL.

venture all he had in the world to secure me. Upon which Richard Penderell came and told me what he had done, at which I was a little troubled; but then there was no remedy, the day being just coming on, and I must either venture that or run some greater danger.

So I came into the house a back way, where I found Mr. Woolfe, an old gentleman, who told me he was very sorry to see me there, because there was two companies of the militia foot at that time in arms in the town, and kept a guard at the ferry, to examine every body that came that way, in expectation of catching some that might be making their escape that way; and that he durst not put me' into any of the hiding-holes of his house, because they had been discovered, and consequently, if any search should be made, they would certainly repair to these holes; and that therefore I had no other way of security but to go into his barn, and there lie behind his corn and hay. So after he had given us some cold meat that was ready, we, without making any bustle in the house, went and lay in the barn all the next day; when, towards evening, his son, who had been prisoner at Shrewsbury, an honest man, was released, and came home to his father's house.   And as soon as ever it began to be a little darkish, Mr. Woolfe and his son brought us meat into the barn; and there we discoursed with them whether we might safely get over the Severn into Wales, which they advised me by no means to adventure upon, because of the strict guards that were kept all along the Severn, where any passage could be found, for preventing any body's escaping that way into Wales.

Upon this I took resolution of going that night the very same way back again to Penderell's house, where I knew I should hear some news what was become of my Lord Wilmot, and resolved again upon going for London.

So we set out as soon as it was dark.   But, as we came by the mill again, we had no mind to be questioned a second time there; and therefore asking Richard Penderell whether he could swim or no, and how deep the river was, he told me it was a scurvy river, not easy to be past in all places, and that he could not swim.   So I told him, that the river being but a little one, I would undertake to help him over.   Upon which we went over some closes to the river side, and I, entering the river first, to see whether I could myself go over, who knew how to swim, found it was but a little above my middle ; and thereupon taking Richard Penderell by the hand, I helped him over.

Which being done, we went on our way to one of Penderell's brothers (his house being not far from White Ladys), who had been guide to my Lord Wilmot, and we believed might, by that time, be come back again ; for my Lord Wilmot intended to go to London upon his own horse. When I came to this house, I inquired where my Lord Wilmot was; it being now towards morning, and having travelled these two nights on foot, Penderell's brother told me that he had conducted him to a very honest gentleman's house, one Mr. Pitchcroft,[1]

[1] The king is mistaken in calling Mr. Whitgrave Mr. Pitchcroft. Pitchcroft is the name of a very large meadow, contiguous to the city of Worcester, where part of the king's troops lay on the night before the battle, and which his majesty might have a distant view of from the top of the tower of the cathedral, where he held a council just before the unfortunate engagement. It is not to be wondered at, if, after the interval of twenty-nine years, the king should mistake the name of a place for the name of a person.— PEPYS.

not far from Woolverhampton,[1] a Roman Catholic.
I asked him, what news? He told me that there
was one Major Careless in the house that was that
countryman; whom I knowing, he having been a
major in our army, and made his escape thither, a
Roman Catholic also, I sent for him into the room
where I was, and consulting with him what we
should do the next day. He told me that it would
be very dangerous for me either to stay in that
house or to go into the wood, there being a great
wood hard by Boscobel; that he knew but one way
how to pass the next day, and that was, to get up
into a great oak, in a pretty plain place, where we
see round about us; for the enemy would certainly
search at the wood for people that had made their
escape. Of which proposition of his I approving,
we (that is to say, Careless and I) went, and carried
up with us some victuals for the whole day—viz.
bread, cheese, small beer, and nothing else, and got
up into a great oak that had been lopt some three
or four years before, and being grown out again,
very bushy and thick, could not be seen through,
and here we staid all the day. I having, in the

1 Mr. Whitgrave lived at Moseley.—Hodi.

meantime, sent Penderell's brother to Mr. Pitch-croft's, to know whether my Lord Wilmot was there or no,[1] and had word brought me by him at night that my lord was there, that there was a very secure hiding-hole in Mr. Pitchcroft's house, and that he desired me to come thither to him.

Memorandum, That while we were in this tree we see soldiers going up and down, in the thicket of the wood, searching for persons escaped, we seeing them now and then peeping out of the wood.

That night Richard Penderell and I went to Mr. Pitchcroft's, about six or seven miles off, where I found the gentleman of the house, and an old grandmother of his, and Father Hurlston,[2] who

[1] I did not depend upon finding Lord Wilmot, but sent only to know what was become of him ; for he and I had agreed to meet at London, at the Three Cranes in the Vintry, and to inquire for Will. Ashburnam.—KING.

[2] His name is Hodlestone, and his grandfather was half brother, by a second venter, to the ancestor of Sir William Hodlestone, who, with eight brothers, raised two regiments for the king, and served with them. Father Hodlestone observes very particularly, as one extraordinary instance of God's providence in this affair, the contingency of his first meeting with John Penderell, occasioned by one Mr. Garret's coming, the Thursday after the fight, out of Warwickshire, from Mrs. Morgan, grandmother to little Sir John

had then the care, as governor, of bringing up two young gentlemen, who, I think, were Sir John Preston and his brother, they being boys.[1]

Here I spoke with my Lord Wilmot, and sent him away to Colonel Lane's,[2] about five or six miles off, to see what means could be found for my escaping towards London; who told my lord, after some consultation thereon, that he had a sister that had a very fair pretence of going hard by Bristol, to a cousin of hers that was married to one Mr. Norton, who lived two or three miles towards Bristol, on Somersetshire side, and she might carry me thither as her man, and from Bristol I might find shipping to get out of England.[3]

Preston, with some new linen for Sir John, and some for Father Hodlestone himself, namely, six new shirts, one whereof he gave to the king, and another to my Lord Wilmot.—HODL.

[1] This Sir John Preston's father was Sir John Preston who raised a regiment for the king, and for so doing had his estate given away by the Parliament to Pen. This Sir John Preston, the son, is since dead, and his estate fallen to his brother, Sir Thomas Preston, mentioned in Oates's narrative of the plot, who married my Lord Molineux his daughter, by whom he had two daughters, great heiresses, himself being become a Jesuit.—PEP.

[2] Colonel Lane lived at Bentley.—HODL.

[3] The king, after having changed his linen and stockings at Mr. Whitgrave's, said, that he found himself at more ease, was

So the next night[1] I went away to Colonel Lane's, where I changed my clothes[2] into a little better habit, like a serving-man, being a kind of gray-cloth suit; and the next day Mrs. Lane and I took our journey towards Bristol, resolving to lie at a place called Long Marson, in the vale of Esham.

But we had not gone two hours on our way but

fit for a new march, and if it would please God ever to bless him with ten or twelve thousand men of a mind, and resolved to fight, he should not doubt but to drive those rogues out of the land.—HODL.

[1] I think I stayed two days at Pitchcroft's [Whitgrave's], but Father Hudlestone can tell better than I.—KING.

[2] The habit that the king came in to Father Hodlestone was a very greasy old gray steeple-crowned hat, with the brims turned up, without lining or hatband, the sweat appearing two inches deep through it, round the band place; a green cloth jump coat, threadbare, even to the threads being worn white, and breeches of the same, with long knees down to the garter; with an old sweaty leathern doublet, a pair of white flannel stockings next to his legs, which the king said were his boot stockings, their tops being cut off to prevent their being discovered, and upon them a pair of old green yarn stockings, all worn and darned at the knees, with their feet cut off; which last he said he had of Mr. Woolfe, who persuaded him thereto, to hide his other white ones, for fear of being observed; his shoes were old, all slashed for the ease of his feet, and full of gravel, with little rolls of paper between his toes, which he said he was advised to, to keep them from galling; he had an old coarse shirt, patched both at the

the mare I rode on cast a shoe ; so we were forced to ride to get another shoe at a scattering village, whose name begins with something like Long——,. And as I was holding my horse's foot, I asked the smith what news. He told me that there was no news that he knew of, since the good news of the beating the rogues of the Scots. I asked him whether there was none of the English taken that joined with the Scots. He answered that he did not hear that that rogue Charles Stuart was taken ; but some of the others, he said, were taken, but not Charles Stuart. I told him, that if that rogue were taken he deserved to be hanged more than

neck and hands, of that very coarse sort which, in that country, go by the name of hogging-shirts ; which shirt, Father Hodlestone shifting from the king, by giving him one of his new ones, Father Hodlestone sent afterwards to Mr. Sherwood, now Lord Abbot of Lambspring, in Germany, a person well known to the Duke [of Yorke], who begged this shirt of Father Hodlestone ; his handkerchief was a very old one, torn, and very coarse, and being daubed with the king's blood from his nose, Father Hodlestone gave it to a kinswoman of his, one Mrs. Brathwayte, who kept it with great veneration, as a remedy for the king's evil ; he had no gloves, but a long thorn-stick, not very strong, but crooked three or four several ways, in his hand ; his hair cut short up to his ears, and hands coloured ; his majesty refusing to have any gloves, when Father Hodlestone offered him some, as also to change his stick.—PEP.

all the rest, for bringing in the Scots. Upon which he said that I spoke like an honest man, and so we parted.

Here it is to be noted, that we had in company with us Mrs. Lane's sister, who was married to one Mr.——, she being then going to my Lord Paget's hard by Windsor, so as we were to part, as accordingly we did, at Stratford-upon-Avon.

But a mile before we came to Stratford-upon-Avon, we espied upon the way a troop of horse,[1] whose riders were alighted, and the horses eating some grass by the way-side, staying there, as I thought, while their muster-master was providing their quarters. Mrs. Lane's sister's husband, who went along with her as far as Stratford, seeing this troop of horse just in our way, said, that for his part he would not go by them, for he had been once or twice beaten by some of the parliament soldiers, and he would not run the venture again. I hearing him say so, begged Mrs. Lane, softly in her ear, that we might not turn back, but go on,

---

[1] A poor old woman that was gleaning in the field cried out, of her own accord, without occasion given her, 'Master, don't you see a troop of horse before you?'—KING.

if they should see us turn. But all she could say in the world would not do, but her brother-in-law turned quite round, and went into Stratford another way. The troop of horse being then just getting on horseback, about twice twelve score off, and, as I told her, we did meet the troop just but in the town of Stratford.

But then her brother and we parted, he going his way, and we ours towards Long Marson, where we lay at a kinsman's, I think, of Mrs. Lane's; neither the said kinsman, nor her afore-mentioned brother-in-law, knowing who I was.

The next night we lay at Cirencester, and so from thence to Mr. Norton's house, beyond Bristol; where as soon as ever I came, Mrs. Lane called the butler of the house, a very honest fellow, whose name was Pope, and had served Tom Jermyn, a groom of my bed-chamber when I was a boy at Richmond, she bade him to take care of William Jackson, for that was my name, as having been lately sick of an ague, whereof she said I was still weak, and not quite recovered. And the truth is, my late fatigues and want of meat had indeed made me look a little pale; besides this, Pope had been a trooper in the king my father's army; but I was not to be known in that house for anything but Mrs. Lane's servant.

Memorandum, That one Mr. Lassells, a cousin of Mrs. Lane's, went all the way with us from Colonel Lane's, on horseback, single, I riding before Mrs. Lane.

Pope the butler took great care of me that night, I not eating, as I should have done, with the servants, upon account of my not being well.

The next morning I arose pretty early, having a very good stomach, and went to the buttery hatch to get my breakfast, where I found Pope and two or three other men in the room, and we all fell to eating bread and butter, to which he gave us very good ale and sack. And as I was sitting there, there was one that looked like a country fellow sat just by me, who, talking, gave so particular an account of the battle of Worcester to the rest of the company, that I concluded he must be one of Cromwell's soldiers. But I asking him, how he came to give so good an account of that battle? He told me he was in the king's regiment, by which I thought he meant one Colonel King's regiment.

But questioning him further, I perceived he had been in my regiment of guards, in Major Broughton's company, that was my major in the battle. I asked him what a kind of man I was? To which he answered by describing exactly both my clothes and my horse; and then looking upon me, he told me that the king was at least three fingers taller than I. Upon which I made what haste I could out of the buttery, for fear he should indeed know me, as being more afraid when I knew he was one of our own soldiers, than when I took him for one of the enemy's.

So Pope and I went into the hall, and just as we came into it Mrs. Norton was coming by through it; upon which I, plucking off my hat, and standing with my hat in my hand as she past by, that Pope looked very earnestly in my face. But I took no notice of it, but put on my hat again, and went away, walking out of the house into the field.

I had not been out half an hour, but coming back I went up to the chamber where I lay; and just as I came thither, Mr. Lassells came to me, and in a little trouble said, 'What shall we do? I am afraid Pope knows you, for he says very positively to me that it is you, but I have denied it.' Upon which I presently, without more ado, asked him whether he was a very honest man or no. Whereto he answering me, that he knew him to be so honest a fellow that he durst trust him with his life, as having been always on our side, I thought it better to trust him, than go away leaving that suspicion upon him; and thereupon sent for Pope, and told him that I was very glad to meet him there, and would trust him with my life as an old acquaintance. Upon which, being a discreet fellow, he asked me what I intended to do; 'for,' says he, 'I am extremely happy I know you, for otherwise you might run great danger in this house. For though my master and mistress are good people, yet there are at this time one or two in it that are very great rogues, and I think I can be useful to you in anything you will command me.' Upon which I told him my design of getting a ship if possible at Bristol; and to that end bade him go that very day immediately to Bristol, to see if there were any ships going either to Spain or France, that I might get a passage away in.

I told him also that my Lord Wilmot was coming

K

to meet me here: for he and I had agreed at Colonel Lane's, and were to meet this very day at Norton's. Upon which Pope told me, that it was most fortunate that he knew me, and had heard this from me, for that if my Lord Wilmot should have come hither, he would have been most certainly known to several people in the house, and therefore he would go. And accordingly went out, and met my Lord Wilmot a mile or two off the house, not far off, where he lodged him till it was night, and then brought him hither by a back door into my chamber, I still passing for a serving-man; and Lassells and I lay in one chamber, he knowing all the way who I was.

So after Pope had been at Bristol to inquire for a ship, but could hear of none ready to depart beyond sea sooner than within a month, which was too long for me to stay thereabout, I betook myself to the advising afresh with my Lord Wilmot and Pope what was to be done. And the latter telling me that there lived somewhere in that country, upon the edge of Somersetshire, at Trent, within two miles of Sherburn, Frank Windham, the knight marshall's brother, who being my old acquaintance, and a very honest man, I resolved to go to his house.

But the night before we were to go away, we had a misfortune that might have done us much prejudice; for Mrs. Norton, who was big with child, fell into labour, and miscarried of a dead child, and was very ill, so that we could not tell how in the world to find an excuse for Mrs. Lane to leave her cousin in that condition; and indeed it was not safe to stay longer there, where there was so great resort of disaffected idle people.

At length, consulting with Mr. Lassells, I thought the best way to counterfeit a letter from her father's house, old Mr. Lane's, to tell her that her father was extremely ill, and commanded her to come away immediately, for fear that she should not otherwise find him alive; which letter Pope delivered so well while they were all at supper, and Mrs. Lane playing her part so dexterously, that all believed old Mr. Lane to be in great danger, and gave his daughter the excuse to go away with me the very next morning early.

Accordingly, the next morning,[1] we went directly

[1] I staid about two days at Pope's [Lassells's].—KING.

to Trent to Frank Windham's house, and lay that night at Castle Cary, and the next night came to Trent, where I had appointed my Lord Wilmot to meet me, whom I still took care not to keep with me, but sent him a little before, or left to come after me.[1]

When we came to Trent, my Lord Wilmot and I advised with Frank Windham whether he had any acquaintance at any sea-town upon the coast of Dorset or Devonshire; who told me that he was very well acquainted with Gyles Strangways, and that he would go directly to him, and inform himself whether he might not have some acquaintance at Weymouth or Lyme, or some of those parts.

But Gyles Strangways proved not to have any, as having been long absent from all those places, as not daring to stir abroad, having been always faithful to the king; but he desired Frank Windham to try what he could do therein, it being unsafe for him to be found busy upon the sea-coast. But withal he sent me three hundred broad pieces, which he knew

---

[1] I ould never get my Lord Wilmot to put on any disguise, he saying that he should look frightfully in it, and therefore did never put on any.—KING.

were necessary for me in the condition I was now in;
for I durst carry no money about me in those mean
clothes, and my hair cut short, but about ten or
twelve shillings in silver.

Frank Windham upon this went himself to Lyme,
and spoke with a merchant there to hire a ship
for my transportation, being forced to acquaint
him that it was I that was to be carried out. The
merchant undertook it, his name being ——, and
accordingly hired a vessel for France, appointing a
day for my coming to Lyme to embark. And
accordingly we set out from Frank Windham's; and,
to cover the matter the better, I rode before a
cousin of Frank Windham's, one Mrs. Judith
Coningsby, still going by the name of William
Jackson.[1]

Memorandum.—That one day, during my stay at
Trent, I hearing the bells ring (the church being
hard by Frank Windham's house), and seeing a
company got together in the churchyard, I sent
down the maid of the house, who knew me, to

[1] At Trent, Mrs. Lane and Lassells went home, I stayed some
four or five days at Frank Windham's house, and was known to
most of his family.—KING.

inquire what the matter was; who returning, came up and told me that there was a rogue a trooper come out of Cromwell's army that was telling the people that he had killed me, and that that was my buff coat which he had then on; upon which, most of the village being fanatics, they were ringing the bells, and making a bonfire for joy of it.

This merchant having appointed us to come to Lyme, we, viz., myself, my Lord Wilmot, Frank Windham, Mrs. Coningsby, and one servant of Frank Windham's, whose name was Peter, were directed from him to a little village hard by Lyme, the vessel being to come out of the cobb at Lyme, and come to a little creek that was just by this village, whither we went, and to send their boat ashore to take us in at the said creek, and carry us over to France, the wind being then very good at north.

So we sat up that night, expecting the ship to come out, but she failed us. Upon which I sent Frank Windham's man, Peter, and my Lord Wilmot, to Lyme the next morning, to know the reason of it. But we were much troubled how to pass away our time the next day, till we could have an answer. At last we resolved to go to a place called Burport, about four miles from Lyme, and there stay till my Lord Wilmot should bring us news whether the vessel could be had the next night or no, and the reason of her last night's failure.

So Frank Windham and Mrs. Coningsby and I went in the morning, on horseback, away to Burport; and just as we came into the town, I could see the streets full of redcoats, Cromwell's soldiers, being a regiment of Colonel Haynes's, viz., fifteen hundred men going to embark to take Jersey, at which Frank Windham was very much startled, and asked me what I would do. I told him that we must go impudently into the best inn in the town, and take a chamber there, as the only thing to be done; because we should otherwise miss my Lord Wilmot, in case we went anywhere else, and that would be very inconvenient both to him and me. So we rode directly into the best inn of the place, and found the yard very full of soldiers. I alighted, and taking the horses, thought it the best way to go blundering in among them, and lead them through the middle of the soldiers into the stable; which I did, and they were very angry with me for my rudeness.

As soon as I came into the stable I took the bridle off the horses, and called the hostler to me to help me, and to give the horses some oats. And as the hostler was helping me to feed the horses, 'Sure, sir,' says the hostler, 'I know your face?' which was no very pleasant question to me. But I thought the best way was to ask him where he had lived—whether he had always lived there or no? He told me that he was but newly come thither; that he was born in Exeter, and had been hostler in an inn there, hard by one Mr. Potter's, a merchant, in whose house I had lain in the time of the war: so I thought it best to give the fellow no further occasion of thinking where he had seen me, for fear he should guess right at last; therefore I told him, 'Friend, certainly you have seen me then at Mr. Potter's, for I served him a good while, above a year.' 'Oh!' says he, 'then I remember you a boy there'; and with that was put off from thinking any more on it, but desired that we might drink a pot of beer together, which I excused by saying that I must go wait on my master, and get his dinner ready for him; but told him that my master was going for London, and would return about three weeks hence, when he would lie there, and I would not fail to drink a pot with him.

As soon as we had dined, my Lord Wilmot came into the town from Lyme, but went to another inn. Upon which we rode out of town, as if we had gone upon the road towards London ; and when we were got two miles off, my Lord Wilmot overtook us (he having observed, while in town, where we were), and told us that he believed the ship might be ready next night, but that there had been some mistake betwixt him and the master of the ship.

Upon which, I not thinking it fit to go back again to the same place where we had sat up the night before, we went to a village called —— —— about four miles in the country above Lyme, and sent in Peter to know of the merchant whether the ship would be ready. But the master of the ship, doubting that it was some dangerous employ- ment he was hired upon, absolutely refused the merchant, and would not carry us over.

Whereupon we were forced to go back again to Frank Windham's to Trent, where we might be in some safety till we had hired another ship.

As soon as we came to Frank Windham's, I sent

away presently to Colonel Robert Philips, who lived then at Salisbury, to see what he could do for the getting me a ship; which he undertook very willingly, and had got one at Southampton, but by misfortune she was, amongst others, prest to transport their soldiers to Jersey, by which she failed us also.

Upon this I sent further into Sussex, where Robin Philips knew one Colonel Gunter, to see whether he could hire a ship anywhere upon that coast. And not thinking it convenient for me to stay much longer at Frank Windham's (where I had been in all about a fortnight, and was become known to very many), I went directly away to a widow gentlewoman's house, one Mrs. Hyde, some four or five miles from Salisbury, where I came into the house just as it was almost dark, with Robin Philips only, not intending at first to make myself known. But just as I alighted at the door, Mrs. Hyde knew me, though she had never seen me but once in her life, and that was with the king my father, in the army, when we marched by Salisbury, some years before, in the time of the war; but she being a discreet woman took no notice at that time of me, I passing only for a friend of Robin Philips, by whose advice I went thither.

At supper there was with us Frederick Hyde, since a judge, and his sister-in-law, a widow, Robin Philips, myself, and Dr. Henshaw, since Bishop of London, whom I had appointed to meet me there.

While we were at supper, I observed Mrs. Hyde and her brother Frederick to look a little earnestly at me, which led me to believe they might know me. But I was not at all startled by it, it having been my purpose to let her know who I was; and accordingly after supper Mrs. Hyde came to me, and I discovered myself to her, who told me she had a very safe place to hide me in, till we knew whether our ship was ready or no. But she said it was not safe for her to trust anybody but herself and her sister, and therefore advised me to take my horse next morning, and make as if I quitted the house, and return again about night; for she would order it so that all her servants and everybody should be out of the house but herself and her sister, whose name I remember not.

So Robin Philips and I took our horses, and

went as far as Stonehenge; and there we staid looking upon the stones for some time,[1] and returned back again to Hale (the place where Mrs. Hyde lived) about the hour she appointed; where I went up into the hiding-hole, that was very convenient and safe, and staid there all alone (Robin Philips then going away to Salisbury) some four or five days.

After four or five days' stay, Robin Philips came to the house, and acquainted me that a ship was ready provided for me at Shoreham by Colonel Gunter. Upon which, at two o'clock in the morning, I went out of the house by the back way, and, with Robin Philips, met Colonel Gunter and my Lord Wilmot together, some fourteen or fifteen miles off, on my way towards Shoreham, and were to lodge that night at a place called Hambleton, seven miles from Portsmouth, because it was too long a journey to go in one day to Shoreham. And here we lay at a house of a brother-in-law

[1] The king and Colonel Phelips rode about the Downes, and took a view of the wonder of the country, Stonehenge; where they found that the king's arithmetic gave the lie to the fabulous tale that those stones cannot be told alike twice together.— PHELIIPS.

of Colonel Gunter's, one Mr. ——, where I was not to be known (I being still in the same grey-cloth suit, as a serving-man), though the master of the house was a very honest poor man, who, while we were at supper, came in, he having been all the day playing the good-fellow at an ale-house in the town, and taking a stool, sat down with us; where his brother-in-law, Colonel Gunter, talking very feelingly concerning Cromwell and all his party, he went and whispered his brother in the ear, and asked whether I was not some round-headed rogue's son, for I looked very suspiciously. Upon which, Colonel Gunter answering for me, that he might trust his life in my hands, he came and took me by the hand, and drinking a good glass of beer to me, called me brother roundhead.

About that time my Lord Southampton, that was then at Titchfield, suspecting, for what reason I don't know, that it was possible I might be in the country, sent either to Robin Philips or Dr. Henshaw to offer his service if he could serve me in my escape. But being then provided of a ship, I would not put him to the danger of having anything to do with it.

The next day we went to a place, four miles off

of Shoreham, called Brighthelmstone, where we
were to meet with the master of the ship, as
thinking it more convenient for us to meet there
than just at Shoreham, where the ship was. So
when we came to the inn at Brighthelmstone, we
met with one [Mansel], the merchant, who had
hired the vessel, in company with her master,[1] the
merchant only knowing me, as having hired her
only to carry over a person of quality that was
escaped from the battle of Worcester, without
naming anybody. And as we were all sitting
together (viz., Robin Philips, my Lord Wilmot,
Colonel Gunter, the merchant, the master, and I),
I observed that the master of the vessel looked very
much upon me. And as soon as we had supped,
calling the merchant aside, the master told him
that he had not dealt fairly with him; for though
he had given him a very good price for the carrying
over that gentleman, yet he had not been clear
with him; 'for,' says he, 'he is the king, and I very
well know him to be so.' Upon which, the merchant denying it, saying that he was mistaken, the

---

[1] Mr. Francis Mansel, the faithful merchant who provided the
bark. Captain Tettershall, the master of the bark.—PHELIPS.

master answered, 'I know him very well, for he .took my ship, together with other fishing vessels at Brighthelmstone, in the year 1648' (which was when I commanded the king my father's fleet, and I very kindly let them go again). 'But,' says he to the merchant, 'be not troubled at it, for I think I do God and my country good service in preserving the king, and, by the grace of God, I will venture my life and all for him, and set him safely on shore, if I can, in France.' Upon which the merchant came and told me what had passed between them, and thereby found myself under a necessity of trusting him. But I took no kind of notice of it presently to him; but thinking it convenient not to let him go home, lest he should be asking advice of his wife, or anybody else, we kept him with us in the inn, and sat up all night drinking beer, and taking tobacco with him.

And here I also run another very great danger, as being confident I was known by the master of the inn; for as I was standing, after supper, by the fireside, leaning my hand upon a chair, and all the rest of the company being gone into another room, the master of the inn came in, and fell a-talking with

me, and just as he was looking about, and saw there
was nobody in the room, he, upon a sudden, kissed
my hand that was upon the back of the chair, and
said to me, 'God bless you wheresover you go! I
do not doubt, before I die, but to be a lord, and my
wife a lady.' So I laughed, and went away into the
next room, not desiring then any further discourse
with him, there being no remedy against my being
known by him, and more discourse might have but
raised suspicion. On which consideration, I thought
it best for to trust him in that manner, and he proved
very honest.

About four o'clock in the morning, myself and
the company before named went towards Shoreham,
taking the master of the ship with us, on horseback,
behind one of our company, and came to the vessel's
side, which was not above sixty ton. But it being
low water, and the vessel lying dry, I and my Lord
Wilmot got up with a ladder into her, and went and
lay down in the little cabin, till the tide came to fetch
us off.

But I was no sooner got into the ship, and lain
down upon the bed, but the master came in to me,
fell down upon his knees, and kist my hand, telling

me that he knew me very well, and would venture
life and all that he had in the world to set me down
safe in France.

So about seven o'clock in the morning, it being
high water, we went out of the port; but the
master being bound for Pool, loaden with sea-coal,
because he would not have it seen from Shoreham
that he did not go his intended voyage, but stood
all the day, with a very easy sail, towards the isle
of Wight (only my Lord Wilmot and myself, of my
company, on board). And as we were sailing, the
master came to me, and desired me that I would per-
suade his men to use their endeavours with me to get
him to set us on shore in France, the better to cover
him from any suspicion thereof. Upon which I went
to the men, which were four and a boy, and told them,
truely, that we were two merchants that had some misfortunes, and were a little in debt; that we had some
money owing us at Rouen, in France, and were afraid
of being arrested in England; that if they would per-
suade the master (the wind being very fair) to give
us a trip over to Dieppe, or one of those ports near
Rouen, they would oblige us very much; and with
that I gave them twenty shillings to drink. Upon

which they undertook to second me, if I would propose it to the master. So I went to the master, and told him our condition, and that if he would give us a trip over to France, we would give him some consideration for it. Upon which he counterfeited difficulty, saying that it would hinder his voyage. But his men, as they had promised me, joining their persuasions to ours, and at last he yielded to set us over.

So about five o'clock in the afternoon, as we were in sight of the Isle of Wight, we stood directly over to the coast of France, the wind being then full north; and the next morning, a little before day, we saw the coast. But the tide failing us, and the wind coming about to the south-west, we were forced to come to an anchor, within two miles of the shore, till the tide of flood was done.

We found ourselves just before an harbour in France called Fescamp; and just as the tide of ebb was made, espied a vessel to leeward of us, which, by her nimble working, I suspected to be an Ostend privateer. Upon which I went to my Lord Wilmot, and telling him my opinion of that ship, proposed to him our going ashore in the little cock-boat, for fear they should prove so, as not knowing but, finding us going into a port of France (there being then a war betwixt France and Spain), they might plunder us, and possibly carry us away and set us ashore in England; the master also himself had the same opinion of her being an Ostender, and came to me to tell me so, which thought I made it my business to dissuade him from, for fear it should tempt him to set sail again with us for the coast of England; yet so sensible I was of it, that I and my Lord Wilmot went both on shore in the cock-boat, and going up into the town of Fescamp, staid there all day to provide horses for Rouen. But the vessel which had so affrighted us proved afterwards only a French hoy.

The next day we got to Rouen, to an inn, one of the best in the town, in the Fishmarket, where they made difficulty to receive us, taking us, by our clothes, to be some thieves, or persons that had been doing some very ill thing, until Mr. Sandburne, a merchant, for whom I sent, came and answered for us.

One particular more there is observable in relation to this our passage into France, that the vessel that brought us over had no sooner landed me, and I given her master a pass, for fear of meeting with any of our Jersey frigates, but the wind turned so happily for her, as to carry her directly for Pool without its being known that she had ever been upon the coast of France.

We staid at Rouen one day, to provide ourselves better clothes, and give notice to the queen, my mother (who was then at Paris), of my being safely landed. After which, setting out in a hired coach, I was met by my mother, with coaches, short of Paris; and by her conducted thither, where I safely arrived.

BY THE PARLIAMENT

A Proclamation for the Discovery and Apprehending of Charles Stuart and other Traytors, his Adherents and Abettors.

WHEREAS CHARLES STUART, Son of the late Tyrant, with Divers of the English and Scottish nation, have lately, in traitorous and hostile Manner, with an Army, invaded this Nation, which, by the Blessing of God upon the Forces of this Commonwealth, have been defeated, and many of the Chief Actors therein slain, and taken Prisoners; but the said CHARLES STUART is escaped : For the speedy apprehending of such a malicious and dangerous Traytor, to the Peace of this Commonwealth, the Parliament doth straitly charge and command all Officers, as well Civil as Military, and all other the good people of this Nation, That they make diligent

Search and Enquiry for the said CHARIES STUART, and his Abettors, and Adherents in this Invasion ; and use their best Endeavours for the Discovery and Arresting the Bodies of them, and every of them ; and being apprehended, to bring, and cause to be brought forthwith and without Delay, in safe Custody, before the Parliament, or Council of State, to be proceeded with and ordered, as Justice shall require : And if any Person shall knowingly conceal the said CHARIES STUART, or any of his Abettors or Adherents, or shall not reveal the Places of their Abode, or Being, if it be in their Power so to do, The Parliament doth declare that they will hold them as Partakers and Abettors of their trayterous and wicked Practices and Designs : And the Parliament doth further publish and declare, That whosoever shall apprehend the Person of the said CHARIES STUART, and shall bring, or cause him to be brought to the Parliament, or Council of State, shall have given and bestowed on him, or them, as a Reward for such Service, the Sum of One Thousand Pounds: And all Officers, Civil and Military, are required to be aiding and assisting unto such Person and Persons therein.   Given at Westminster this Tenth

Day of September, One Thousand Six Hundred Fifty-one.

Ordered by the Parliament, That this Proclamation be forthwith Printed and Published.

HEN. SCOBEL, *Cler. Parl.*

LONDON : Printed by JOHN FIELD, Printer to the Parliament of England.   1651.

EDINBURGH

T. & A. CONSTABLE

Printers to Her Majesty

1894

THE

MEMORIAL LIBRARY EDITION

OF THE WORKS OF THE IATE

SIR RICHARD F. BURTON.

———◆———

I. A PERSONAL NARRATIVE OF A PILGRIMAGE TO
AL-MADINAH AND MECCAH. Memorial Edition. *Complete.*
Carefully revised from the Author's own Copy, and containing all
the original coloured Illustrations, and Maps, and Plans, and also
the Wood-cuts from the later Editions. With photogravure portrait
of Lady Burton, as Frontispiece. *In Two vols. Price* TWEIVE
SHIIIINGS, *net.*

'The brilliant narrative reads as vividly as ever. . . . We are glad to see his
books revived in a form worthy of their intrinsic merit.'—*Athenæum.*

'As a mere book of travel and adventure it is excellent, and it is besides shot
through with humour.'—*Manchester Guardian.*

'Few stories of adventure have the interest of Sir Richard Burton's vigorous
narrative, and fewer still have its literary and ethnographic value. . . . One of
the most marvellous records of daring ever penned. . . . We heartily recommend
the Memorial Edition of the Pilgrimage.'—*Publishers' Circular.*

'Every credit is due to the publishers for what they have done towards
making paper, printing, binding, and those dozen matters which are included
in the one term "get up," worthy of the book and worthy of the author.'—
Graphic.

'Two most fascinating volumes ; the richness and magic of which it is only
possible to realise by reading them—as every one must, who once takes them
up—from beginning to end.'—*Star.*

'The book is one of extraordinary interest, and well repays purchase and
perusal.'—*Manchester Courier.*

'It is a fascinating story, not only picturesquely told, but revealing on every
page a personality more interesting than anything that the said personality ever
wrote.'—*Daily Graphic.*

'It will be impossible in a paragraph or two to give any adequate idea of the
mass of information and entertainment it contains.'—*Saturday Review.*

'Every episode is so vividly described that the reader is compelled to follow the story with increasing interest, and cannot fail to obtain, almost unconsciously, a vast amount of valuable information.'—*Dundee Advertiser.*

'Burton never wrote anything more captivating. Those who excite and incite like him, and make a ceiling and stone walls a prison while you read, are rare, just as rare as he was himself.'—*Sketch.*

'This is one of those books which, when once read, are never forgotten, and are always re-read with pleasure.'—*St. James's Budget.*

'Even Burton never wrote anything better than his "Pilgrimage to Mecca." After years one's appetite returns to it, and on a second reading one is more than ever struck by the amount of marvel and of peril which he takes for granted, and mentions as mere circumstance. It is a great book of travels.'—*Bookman.*

'The narative is one of absorbing interest. . . . Those who know the book of old will welcome the present handsome edition, and those who do not know it may be congratulated on the pleasure in store for them.'—*Glasgow Herald.*

II. A MISSION TO GELELE, KING OF DAHOME.

Memorial Edition. *Complete.* With Frontispieces. *In Two vols.* Price Tweive Shiiiings, *net.*

'Of all Burton's books this account of his hazardous mission to Dahomey is one of the least known; it brings out, in a very marked manner, the writer's unfailing tact and resource in dealing with savage peoples.'—*Daily Graphic.*

'Carefully edited and excellently got up.'—*Glasgow Herald.*

'The style is more colloquial than that of the "Pilgrimage to Mecca," but it is none the less readable and attractive. The effect produced by the book is that of a clever man talking over his adventures after dinner, or in a club smoking-room.'—*Manchester Guardian.*

'An uncompromising account of a race which has, perhaps, been sentimentalised over more than any other.'—*Star.*

'The republication of Sir R. Burton's "Mission to Gelele, King of Dahomey," is seasonable, seeing that public interest in that country has been revived by the recent operations of French troops.'—*Manchester Examiner and Times.*

'Among the multifarious works of Sir Richard Burton, this monograph on the kingdom of Dahomey holds its place as a proof of the author's inveterate love of travelling, of his searching insight into native habits, of his capabilities as a public servant, and of his frank and uncompromising expression of his own opinions regardless of the prejudices of others.'—*Publishers' Circular.*

'In view of the French projects these volumes appear very opportunely, and are in themselves, as a record of an embassy to a very unconventional potentate, among the most interesting of Sir Richard's strange and varied experiences.'— *The Literary World.*

'His expedition may be regarded as the first opening up of the interior of this part of Africa to European enterprise.'—*Dundee Advertiser.*

'Now that the affairs of Dahomey are frequently attracting attention, these volumes are very timely. How exceedingly interesting they are our extracts will have sufficed to show.'—*St. James's Budget.*

III. VIKRAM AND THE VAMPIRE: Taies of Hindu Deviiry. Memorial Edition. *Complete.* With 33 Illustrations by Ernest Griset. *In One vol. Price* Six Shiiiings, *net.*

There is also a large paper edition of this book, printed on Arnold's unbleached hand-made paper, in royal 8vo, limited to 200 copies, which, in addition, contains a new photogravure Frontispiece by Albert Letchford, and in which the sixteen full-page plates are printed on special China paper and mounted. *Price* Twenty-five Shiiiings, *net.*

'Strange, humorous, and fascinating stories.'—*Echo.*

'A book which is fascinating in the extreme, and if there yet remains any lover of the fantastic and picturesque in literature who has not read these enchanting tales, let us hasten to assure him that he has a most delightful experience in store.'—*St. James's Budget.*

'As a "creepy" story-book and picture-book, this "Vikram" is not easy to beat.'—*National Observer.*

'It is an amusing book, a strange mixture of philosophy and nonsense.'— *Liverpool Post.*

'Fantastic (tales) all of them, gruesome many of them; full of strange, witty inventions; their very grotesqueness fascinates, while their applicability to modern times fills one with wondering.'—*Bookman.*

'It is a volume of fascinating interest to the student of things Oriental, and is written with all that charm of style of which Burton was so consummate a master.'—*Publishers' Circular.*

'Rather strong meat.'—*Globe.*

'Can hold its own with any of those stories of myth and mystery which are so especially characteristic of the East.'—*The Literary World.*

'Full of witty strokes and points of comic devilment.'—*Scotsman.*

'Stories you cannot begin without reading to the very end.'—*Star.*

IV. FIRST FOOTSTEPS IN EAST AFRICA. Memorial Edition. *Complete.* With 2 Maps and 4 Coloured Illustrations. *In Two vols. Price* TWEIVE SHIIIINGS, *net.*

'A perusal of this acceptable reprint recalls once more Burton's admirable qualities as a writer, and his supreme resource as a discoverer.'—*National Observer.*

'"First Footsteps in East Africa" is a most exciting narrative—the marvellous record of a marvellous man, whose real greatness, though ungrudgingly recognised in many quarters, has never been so universally acknowledged as it ought to be.'—*Sheffield Daily Telegraph.*

'Burton was really the last of the great travellers. All who care for East African topics should read his narrative.'—*Echo.*

'For dauntless bravery this was, perhaps, the most daring exploit that Burton ever attempted.'—*Dundee Advertiser.*

'As a tale of adventure and exploration it scarcely yields to the author's famous journey to Mecca.'—*Scotsman.*

'The narrative of the long, weary, and perilous expedition to the Dreadful City, of the ten days which his capacity for passing as an Arab enabled him to spend in it, and of the terrible journey back to Berberah, is as stirring as anything in fiction.'—*Glasgow Herald.*

'The whole narrative is a model for all travellers, and one is delighted to have an excuse for renewing acquaintance with it.'—*Daily Graphic.*

'It is altogether a delightful book.'—*Pall Mall Gazette.*

The above Volumes, which are demy octavo in size, printed from new type, on good paper, and tastefully bound in black and gold, will be followed from time to time by other Works of SIR RICHARD BURTON, of which due notice will be given.

EACH WORK IS SOLD SEPARATELY.

MESSRS. TYLSTON AND EDWARDS, PUBLISHERS, 13 CLIFFORD'S INN, LONDON, E.C.

THIS BOOK IS DUE ON THE LAST DATE STAMPED BELOW

AN INITIAL FINE OF 25 CENTS

WILL BE ASSESSED FOR FAILURE TO RETURN THIS BOOK ON THE DATE DUE. THE PENALTY WILL INCREASE TO 50 CENTS ON THE FOURTH DAY AND TO $1.00 ON THE SEVENTH DAY OVERDUE.

s b

NOV 28 1936

OCT 7 1940 M

en

REG. CIR. JAN 26 '78

NOV 1 1937

22 Apr'49 GP

11 May 49 DJ

OCT 19 1938

25 May'49 III B

JAN 23 1939

11 May'59 WW

FEB 6 1939

RECD LD

2 - 6

McConnell

MAY 1

FEB 16 1939

2 Dec'62 RA